T0193362

SUHAIL S. JARROUSH Ph.D.

WHAT WOULD THIS OLD MAN SAY

Do not ask me how to let go,
Tell me why you are holding on.

authorHOUSE

AuthorHouse™
1663 Liberty Drive
Bloomington, IN 47403
www.authorhouse.com
Phone: 1 (800) 839-8640

Published by AuthorHouse 01/08/2020

ISBN: 978-1-7283-4035-7 (sc)
ISBN: 978-1-7283-4034-0 (hc)
ISBN: 978-1-7283-4038-8 (e)

Library of Congress Control Number: 2019920896

Print information available on the last page.

CONTENTS

"Think my little wandering star, a name Steven used to always call me by, think of what you are saying. Do not fire your words with the instinct of the wolf, nor with the passion of the hawk, or the intimidation of a lamb; but create a balance between your thoughts and expressions, your logic, your passion and your love and I promise you that your words will someday create wonders".

-**Steven**, *My Spiritual Teacher*

Why the old man?

14 years ago in 2005, Melissa a younger student of mine who became the daughter I never had, called me in public "My Old Man" Not that I am very old, but she referred to a wise old man on a TV show (kung Fu). Since then, this great title stuck with me, and she became my Grasshopper.

DEDICATION

To Steven, my spirit teacher and my guide who opened my eyes to freedom of thought and the power to be; to Maryam my angle and my protector; to my wife, my love and my dearest friend, Amal, the gentle soul who put up with my craziness and became the back bone of my stability in this life time; to Suzanne my student, my partner and my companion who journeyed with me through many lives relentlessly pushing me to write this book; to my son Joseph-Salim whose life inspired the best in me; to the souls of my father and mother (Salim and May) who are constantly engaged in love, to my brother Sami and sister Giselle my companions in this earthly journey, to all my godchildren, and grandchildren, whose births illuminated my old spirit; to all my nephews and nieces who brought me joy and happiness; to all my close buddies and all my students who taught me as I taught them; and to every person who constantly ask "who am I and how can I let go?", I dedicate this book.

PREFACE

I have been driven for years to write this book. It has gone through many transformations because I did not want this to be like any other self-help book out there. I am not writing this book to tell people how to grow, change their lives or to let go. I am writing this book to tell everyone that the power to modify the self is a power within each one of us to create ourselves the way we choose to develop, not the way we have been told to be. I am sharing my personal growth from an inquisitive child to the adult I am today to show all that even though we may come from different backgrounds we all have the power to recreate the self the way we choose to be.

I have been asked by many students and colleagues to write this book. Truly, there is no one way to find the truth for the truth resides within each one of you. You and only you have the power to let go when you decide to stop holding on. You are all diamonds in the rough, but you all have the power to become well cut brilliant shining diamonds by the creative power within each one of you.

You are life, not a student of life. You may believe that your life is a result of a physical joining of a sperm and an egg, and your living is a result of your random experiences. The truth is, you are the Master that creates the force of life. You alone arrange the experience of living in order to affirm your divine self and create your earthly existence with the grandest feelings you could ever imagine. "On earth as it is in heaven".

Life is the energy force for living at every stage of being. Energy changes its form and vibration, but energy never dies. Death of a certain vibration is not the end; it is simply a beginning of a different vibration. Life changes its form to match the realm in which it is experiencing itself in different structures, but life's energy never dies. As the energy of your spirit changes form when it enters the union of a sperm and an egg in your mother's womb to begin the experience of a physical living by forming a human body in an environment of water giving this new creation all that is necessary for this experience. Then when the time to complete the building of the physical body is completed, that existence dies or transforms from living in water to be born to the next experience of becoming an air breathing human living in a physical world. This new physical world, with all its physical challenges and Judgements, becomes in its turn the experiments needed for a human to affirm its grandest feelings through the illusion of a physical life as a reality.

Then when the allotted time to complete this mission expires, the spirit dies to the physical illusion and is born to the third phase of developing the mind power. But if the time in physical expires and the spirit did not achieve the grandest feelings while in the physical illusion, it will not be able to move into the realm of the mind. The whole process of living in water to develop a physical body and living in the physical illusion will be repeated until a success is achieved. Then truly, it behooves us to succeed in the physical allotted time to affirm the grandest feelings we can be in while living the physical illusion as humans.

– **Suhail S. Jarroush**
The Old Man

ACKNOWLEDGEMENTS

Testimonials written by students

Suhail, your classes as well as the time spent one on one with you have been moments in my life that I will treasure forever. I am also grateful for our friendship. Your guidance and support through this mystery we call life has been amazing and I am truly grateful for you. Your classes have helped me discover a better version of myself. I look at all the courses as one process of self-discovery and all the things I learned from you have merged into one understanding. And that is that I am a representation of the divine. When I slip into periods of anxiety or stress, I simply affirm that knowing, and my worries quickly disappear. Thank You!

- Nick S.

Taught with charismatic style and a unique perspective, Dr. Jarroush's classes led me to some mind-blowing revelations that, for certain broadened my horizons. Now, I know that I have everything I need to create my own solutions and I understand how to access that power within! Thank you, Suhail, for providing the encouragement and surety that I can take control of any emotion, situation and event, and raise my level of being and opportunity!"

Dear Suhail, I extend my deepest gratitude to you, Old Man. You are one of the special people who were put on my path to educate, mentor, guide and help me realize my true potential. You have helped me understand that healing, growth, self-love, and forgiveness are essential in life. The lessons and experiences are priceless to me. Thanks for always being there. It is truly a blessing to share this lifetime with you.

With Love
- Katarzyna G.

Dear Suhail, I met you in 2008. I still remember our first conversation. I had a lot on my mind. The one-hour time that I blocked with you was long gone, but I still had a lot to talk. You did not display any signs that you are in a rush or wanted me gone. So, I decided to continue… back of my mind I was thinking, it is gonna cost me a lot, but I was willing to pay any price because it was a good conversation and your participation was sincere. After three hours, I had a sigh of relief and you had a big smile, and the money part, you said "you owe me nothing". I spent three hours for the first time with a counselor and he charges me nothing, I knew I found my teacher. A teacher who is genuine!

Rest is history. In this past 11 years, I learnt, I grew, and I am still doing it. From the meditations to Reiki shares, to Self-Empowerment courses to hypnotherapy classes, it's all been an awesome journey. Your Guidance, motivation and support has been very instrumental in shaping who I am today. Back in 2008, from the many listings of Google Search, I chose you because Suhail is my favorite name and I am glad for it.

Thank you for everything!!!
Love & Regards
- Ameena V.

I have known and worked with Dr. Suhail S. Jarroush "the Old Man" on a personal and professional basis for over 10 years. I have seen all kind of miracles from this human being on how he helps people to get rid of their physical, emotional, mental and spiritual pain. I have received all kinds of wisdom/training from Dr. Jarroush that I use on daily basis that has made my life peaceful, happy and free. Suhail "The old man" has shown me the most effective ways to release my personal feeling of anger, stress, fear and anxiety whenever I am facing life situations, and it brings out old stories from the past. I have exchanged energy thousands of times with this human through the heart, and I have seen and felt things that you cannot describe on this earth because there are no words to truly explain it.

- Donna H.

Good Morning! Suhail and his teachings have opened my eyes to living a more satisfying and meaningful life. I met Suhail in 2005 as I was searching: searching for freedom from my frustrations, searching for happiness, searching for love and peace. It was time for me to invest in myself and make some sense from my chaos. After a few brief encounters with Suhail, I decided to become his student.

It was the turning point of my life.

Suhail is the Old Man who inspires us to find answers. His methods of questioning and exploration have taught me see to the many more facets of a story, a decision, or a struggle. To this day, Suhail continues to spark my curiosity and elevates me to find my own successes. His wisdom has given me power to enrich my relationships, my career, and my view of the world.

Make no mistake, self-exploration is a challenge. It takes time. It will hurt: physically, emotionally, mentally, spiritually. Suhail is here to guide with light, to guard with strength, and to encourage with heart.

- Melissa B.

INTRODUCTION

"I am so confused. I read so many books and all said I must change; I must let go. I am here in your class now; please tell me how I can change? How I can let go?"

a student passionately addressed me with tears in her eyes as she attended the beginners Self-Awareness class in my powerful Self-Discovery Series. I looked at her tears with so much compassion. She reminded me of all the people that came to me through the years to ask the same question that never changed *"how can I let go?"* I cracked a smile and answered her as I have answered so many for years; do not ask me how to let go, ask yourself why you are still holding on. To be able to accomplish this simple majestic liberating task, you must discover yourself. You must discover the inborn power you possess. Hang on my dear hang on; it is a discovery process that you will shortly engage all parts of your existence to fulfill. You will understand, express and empower yourself to become. You will soon learn that all the power you seek to help you change is all within you. You will soon be able to stand in front of the mirror, salute yourself and say: Mission Accomplished. I am now free.

Self-Discovery my friends is the grandest story of individual human triumph over their conscious physical domination. It is a story that all humanity aches to write at one time or another. It is the single mission of creation you and every human born to this earth is meant to fulfill. It is the story of Awareness, Expression and Empowerment that makes you and every human live "on earth as it is in heaven". It is the story that drops the self-made impotent veils of ignorance, confusion, slavery, insignificance, mediocrity, fear, abandonment, obligation and judgment, to uncover the majestic simple face of truth. These self-made veils of self-ignorance and constant self-dependence on some authority to guide our steps in living becomes the catalyst of our values and beliefs. Our acceptance of the relentless bombardment and persistent programming by societies, parents, religions, schools, economic status, geographical affiliations, political orientations suffocate us and impair our insights from recognizing the single reason for being born to this earth. And that reason once again is to do what matters to experience and live "on earth as it is in heaven".

So, what does live on earth as it is heaven mean? How do we liberate ourselves? What is the way to drop these blinding veils and perform what matters to complete this simple but grand assignment? How do we start to break away from the chains of our habits, and the bondage of our belief systems? How do we know if we are on the right path? What is this spirituality that if we follow our lives will change for the better? What is better? Is it to simply attain what we lack? It seems every life-changing teacher today talks about spirituality in such mysterious ways, using words and sentences from far India, China and Tibet as if spirituality has been created only for certain life-trained gurus from some temples of obedience in the Far East, which we are supposed to imitate. Is Spirituality a trade's mark of the Far East which we must buy like gadgets, toys and watches? Is Spirituality a simple repetition of some Sanskrit words and bowing to each other while we do not comprehend what we are saying, but simply imitating some enlightened guru that truly knows what he is saying and why he is doing what he is doing, while wearing strange attires with long unattended beards and some jingling beads? Why we cannot be spiritual wearing our suits and clean shaven and learn the power that the teacher has, rather than just mimicking him to attain our own spirituality?

Something is missing in here. We follow Eastern Yoga, Eastern Reiki and Eastern Chi Masters to understand Spirituality, and all we do is to imitate what the Chinese, Koreans, Japanese and Tibetans do chanting words that we do not comprehend or most of the time cannot pronounce, while we struggle with our understanding of our own religions, ways and inherited understanding of Deity. Why only an oriental Master can put his foot around his neck while chanting mysterious words that we must repeat if we choose to be spiritual? Is Spirituality an Eastern invention, or is it the affirmation of the Spirit that everyone born to this earth does already possess? Is it that we are bored with our Gods, Angels and Demons and we seek new deity just for a change, and good luck? Is it that what we have been repeating in our prayers from the day we were born is not helping us to seek some freedom? Why are our ways not spiritual? We have been blessed with land of milk and honey the whole world envy us for what we can create, while the East with its self-proclaimed spirituality is the cradle of poverty, lack and misery. Why is it that these great enlightened masters do not teach their grand ways of spirituality and enlightenment to their own people, but instead they create spinning chakra wheels on their behalf so that their prayers can reach heaven? The grandest question we should ask now is why we in the west are so mechanically, logically, self-preservation oriented and self-survival saturated that we forgot our spiritual power, which in turn compels us to go buy a replica from the Orient?

Hang in there my friends; in the pages that follow, we will together dissect the so-called mysterious secrets of Spirituality and Self Discovery. I will guide your steps to accomplish what you always thought is so beyond your reach. We will engage in simple steps that any one of you with any resolve to understand and grow can follow. As you move through this book many mysterious secrets of living are uncovered through series of questions and answers that many of my students, throughout the years have repeatedly asked.

Also, within these chapters you will hear my own simple story of Self-Discovery. The story that changed me a young rebellious child from the mountains of Lebanon, that now resides for the past 45 years in the USA, who carried the guilt of my grandfather's death throughout my childhood, and could not accept the ever changing rules that people imposed on me, and the vain regulations of the same religious answers as a response to my dilemmas, anger and frustration. I questioned God and his angels, the Devil and all his demons, the injustice of civil establishments and the tyranny of religions and its men. I could not understand my confusion. I asked a million questions and found no answers in organized religion, in the school system, in social injustice, and especially at home. I prayed to God and got no answer. I searched the sacred books and listened to Sufi hakims, educated gurus, clerics and common monks, and got no answer. I engaged my parents, my teachers, the priests and bishops, the oracles, the soothsayers, the psychics, the tarot cards readers and yet found no straight answer; until the day I met my spirit guide (Steven), the teacher of my dreams, who showed me how to see with my insight rather than relying on my eyes only to see. He led me by his love. He did not teach me how to let go, but rather he taught me how to drop the heavy, old and obsolete stories that I was still holding on to.

From that moment of truth, and through the tunnel of time, the story shifted with the winds of wisdom. This child's life changed from a fearful child to a teacher of men and women. I changed from a confused young man to a spiritual teacher and guide, helping students all-over-the-world to become aware of the power of the Divine Mind of solutions they have within them. I engaged and challenged them to see that every human on this earth has the capacity to create a new grand feeling of majesty and divinity regardless of the situation, experience, test, situation or event they might face. Like diamonds in the rough, I helped them remove their excess debris unveiling the luster of their hearts, which guided their steps to live "on earth as it is in heaven"

Though now an older man, the child within me still asks questions. But my questions changed from how to deal with life's problems to how to create new perceptions to every problem. My reality altered from how to cope with a chocking experience and its outcome, to how to create new conscious solutions to the same experience, causing its outcome to vanish, and thus letting go of its effect. My attitude changed from being a victim of circumstances, society, religion, people and destiny, to a master of my own destiny; a preordained destiny of my own creation where nothing is done to me from birth to death, but all my experiences and the way I feel are done by me. My life changed from blinding confusion to the total awareness of letting go to create new realities of the grandest vision of who I choose to be. I dared to stand alone and shout through the tunnel of time I am free. My God, My God nothing separates me from you except my ignorance. I am grateful for my opportunity on this earth. Thank you, thank you for always being with me. Thank you for allowing me to know that I am a branch of your tree, and my divinity is your divine. My steps moved from living life as it was dictated to me, to creating a living of my own design and choices; where the outcome of an experience makes no difference as long as the power of the balance is the norm. My question changed from how do I let go? To why am I holding on?

The child within the man is now free. I reinvented myself and I Let Go. I now travel through the tunnel of time with gratitude for the opportunity to teach, holding my brush and drawing my story on the canvas of space and time. I install this spirit of power, self-freedom and Oneness with God in the hearts of all my students as they become masters of their own destinies, holding their brushes in their own hands, and drawing their part of the story on the canvas of their living. They still look up towards me (sometimes) for guidance, they call me the Old Man; but I still look forward to my nights with Steven, my spirit guide now, and to the multitude of my spirit friends for debates, empowerment and growth.

Throughout this book, the story moves through various questions and answers ranging from the essence of being to the simple act of letting go. Essential Basic tools will be introduced to help you liberate yourself from the yoke of slavery to thoughts, feelings and emotions installed in you by your past lives, religion, family, your socio-economic status and your geo-political dwelling. You will discover simple tools to help you break the chains of self-doubt, anger, worry, guilt, fear, jealousy, need, want, and depression. You will be amazed by the power of simplicity that these plain tools pack. You will, if you are willing to open your mind and heart, understand spirituality as the sharpest focused force of the mind you can willfully direct to empower you to live life the way you choose it to be, rather than living your life hating yourself and all that you do not want to be.

As you read on, you will discover your power to affirm grand feelings you always had. You will also discover simple tools that will assist you in achieving your goals in life. You will finally let go of what was, and you will begin the journey of Self-Discovery creating your living on earth as it is in heaven.

Open your heart and let your mind bring new solutions, and I will guarantee you that your life will forever change.

CHAPTER ONE

WAVES OF CHAOS

"How can I just let go" She screamed at me, "Children are not supposed to die before their parents, where is this compassionate God of love and mercy you keep talking about? He is an f##kn murderous God that hates me? Why did he do this to me, why? She screamed at the top of her lungs as she dropped to her knees trying to wipe her burning tears and her nose with her sleeve; Is this a punishment for something bad I have done? How can I endure this? How can I just let go? Please help me".

I touched her shoulder with compassion as I felt and understood her pain. The words tumbled out of my mouth as it usually happens when I get tongue tied and my friends start to talk through me. It is not a punishment by a sadistic God. The death of your son was not done to you. God did not arrange for your misery; but in your sadness for the loss of your son, you misunderstood the experience that you went through and labeled it as an act of murder and revenge. For now, my dear, take a deep breath, in through your nose and out through your mouth and relax; for soon you will learn, soon you will discover for yourself the power that this experience had developed within you. But for now, mourn my friend the loss of your son if need be, but do not mourn his death. Soon you will understand that death truly does not exist. Your son is alive in a different form. But for now, calm down, and let your tears flow for soon you will remember, and you will understand.

I looked at my student's face and stood still. My life flashed in front of me for seconds that felt like a life's long drama. I traveled in a flash back to the days of my early youth where I constantly heard the words I just uttered to my student ringing in my head; a time of my childhood where the idea of death used to shackle me with fear, and the injustice of dying choked every breath I could take. I remembered the dream that haunted my being for years, I saw myself as a barely 10 year old in my bed, and heard my own voice pleading with God to make me understand.

I heard my trembling voice faintly approaching from the distant past pleading with God. My God, my God, I beg you talk to me. When will this confusion end? Oh God!!! I am scared. Why does my inside tremble? Why I am shaking? Why I cannot breathe? Oh Lord what is this death? Why do I have to die? Why did my Grandfather die? Is it because I lied to my aunt, God punished me by killing my Grandfather? The priest in the morning mass said that we pay for our sins with death. What the hell is sin? Why do I have to suffer for what the priest said is an original sin? Why do my parents keep feeding me apples, when Adam's sin as the priest said was eating an apple? Am I going to be punished and die some day for lying to my aunt when she asked me about what I knew? Why did God kill my grandfather for my lie? What is this crooked justice? When would this nightmare end? Why am I so delirious? Was I born only to die? Why Does God enjoy Killing people? Oh God, do you enjoy my pain? Did you create me to torture me, to see me suffer and die? Or What…? What is your problem my dear God? Why was I born and why must I die? Where did I come from and where must I go? Why do we have to go from our mother's belies to a hole in the ground? Or is there something else?

Did I really kill my grandfather because I lied? I felt the world spinning around me. I could not find an answer. It came to me in dreams. It came to me in daytime. The worst feeling was the thought that because of me, worms were eating my grandfather. Where is the truth oh God, and where can I find it? I am suffocating with fear my God, please help me.

Then God with God's divine mercy like a breeze from heaven gently touched my forehead. I heard a gentle female voice purer than the whisper of the breeze calming my raging soul, heavenly fingers brushing through the back of my hair. Gentle warmth replaced the chill in my spine. My eyes closed. A tear left my eyelids, burned its trail as it trickled down my cheek and landed on my pillow. I heard God's soothing voice echoing through my head saying: "Sleep my child. Sleep in peace. Soon all will be clear, soon a teacher will come, and you will be able to see".

I regained my senses standing in class as I felt the heavenly fingers of Maryam the Goddess of heaven (My heavenly mother, protector and guide) brushing her fingers through what is left of my hair, and her gentle whisper urging me to attend to my class. I looked at my student and said: There is no beginning, there is no end. There is no birth, and there is no death. It is a continuous cycle of life and living, though in different forms and personalities, but it is all the same route and each one of us is trying to clear a part of this illusion that we call humanity.

What do you mean there is no beginning and no end? What are you saying? We all know we are born, and we must die. I cannot understand this philosophical talk, another student fired at me. *I thought I was confused when I came into class, now I am sure I am confused. I do not understand what you are saying. I must be stupid or unqualified to be in this class.*

I smiled at her and said: I am sorry my dear, you are really qualified to be in this class of life. There are no stupid students, only stupid teachers that cannot relay the message in a way that even a child could understand. My Student smiled, calmed down and sat ready to listen.

I looked at a new group attending the beginners Self-Awareness class and for a moment my mind traveled through the years and the many questions that students asked me throughout those years.

What is Death? What is Birth? Why are we born? What is suffering? What is fear? What is Anger? What is guilt? What is a victim? What is an experience? What is a test? Who is God? What is sin? What is the devil? What makes a human? What is the difference between all creations? What is fair? What is justice? What is the kingdom of God? What is religion? What is spirituality? Why can't I get all I want? What is prayer? What is meditation? Is there more of me than what I see in the mirror? What is incarnation? What is heaven? What is hell? Who are the angels? Who are the demons? What is mercy? Why is the God of Creation completely different from the God of the New Testament? How many Gods are there? But the most prominent of them all is *How can I let go? How can I start again?*

I rested in my chair during the break cradling my head. My mind soared back to my youth and the million questions that always haunted my living came dashing through my senses as if to compete with questions that my students ask. Though I have answers to all my old questions now, the child within this Old Man that lived on the slopes of Mount Lebanon still loves to play the game of wits with Steven my spiritual guide. Though I now have great tools to get rid of the child's worries, I decided to keep that rebel within me to remind me of what questions would I face from my students.

As I rested in my chair for a moment, the child within rushed. His first question was, *did I kill my grandfather? Is he food for worms? Or is he living?*

If he is alive, how come his body is in the grave? Where is the answer? Then I heard Steven, my spiritual guide, come in to say: Come on little Wondering Star, you should know better by now. Your innocent lie did not kill your grandfather. It was his time to leave, and his anger was the tool he used to exit this life and go back home. The child sprang up to say: *Steven you asked me to read the bible, I read it, but it did not make any sense... too many conflicting stories. All that I understood was that God is not just. God shows favoritism to some people over the entire world. What kind of God is this? Where is that God you asked me to talk to while praying? Why doesn't he talk to me?* Steven Chuckled as usual and said: God talks to you every moment of your living time, and then more, but in your fury you do not listen. *Why did he allow my grandfather to die? Why does he create people, and why does he kill them? Is death a game God enjoys playing? Does he enjoy going to his hunting grounds?* Then Steven in the calmness of his soul said: God is not a criminal. God's creative power does not breed people to kill them. God created humans so that people can affirm their own creative power. God gave humanity a physical body and a free will to affirm their grandest form to experience the thrill of the experience. But humans chose to make the earth a permanent home and forgot the reason for which they were born. I know my little Wondering Star it is a bit difficult for you to understand now, but that will be your mission in living, and to the end of your earthly life, your mission is to live and remind humanity of this reality.

I came back to my senses as I felt the hand of Suzanne my partner touching my shoulder saying: *Suhail it is time to start the class again.*

CHAPTER TWO

BEND YOUR MATRIX

Before we go any deeper in understanding the self and use powerful tools to fix your ways, you must understand basic meanings and simple explanations about who are you. So, I am going to ask your honest participation in telling me basic deep issues you are living through in your daily living. Basic question that all humans ask at one time or another in their daily living. Questions such as: Why you live with all these conflicting feelings in your daily living.

A voice came from a student sitting next to me:

Why was I born? What is the purpose of me being on this earth when I will die at some time or another?

Another question came flying from the back: *Why am I afraid? Why Am I always afraid of what might happen next? Why do I always feel guilty? Why do I have constant conflict within me that I am always wrong, always doing something that someone I deal with believes I should not have done. Why do I feel ashamed of things I did? Why does my religious upbringing confuse me, and it does not meet my expectations anymore?* Another student asked

Other questions came flying in from different students:

Why am I always grieving for my loss? Why do I always lie to myself, why do I have false beliefs? Why Do I always live in a state of illusion, pretending That I am well, when I am feeling miserable inside. How can I empower myself to achieve the grandest feeling I could ever be in regardless of the experience I am facing?

Before I start to answer these powerful questions and concerns, let me start by saying in order to answer any of your questions to yourself, you must be ready to bend your Matrix or change your own way of retaining and dealing with your judgements and habits that you imprisoned within your own beliefs in system or Matrix of your own creation. Personal beliefs involving your motivations, emotions, learnings, emotional memories, moods, sexuality, bonding, stress, anxiety and depression.

You must learn how to empower yourself by engaging your mind's power, wisdom and love to live in your consciousness and thinking. It is your process that enables you to reason, think, feel, will, perceive, judge and be aware of your experiences.

The secret to Self-Empowerment is to face your own fears and demons, then develop the courage to realize the fine line between the reality of your expressions, and the illusion of your fears. Those choking demons of fear that you have created within yourself in this life, and those you brought with you from other past lives.

First, you must eliminate the false, negative and outdated beliefs that support the "status quo" that bring your beliefs of obligations, expectations, limitations and regulations that hold you in bondage to a living that chokes you. Self-Empowerment is a creative process, based on the combination of your physical, emotional, mental and spiritual beliefs that you create throughout all the stages of your life.

7

The second step is to create the empowered person you wish to become by downloading a new belief system that supports living a genuine life based on affirming the grandest feelings of divinity. As much as we all want to restart our living as a blank canvas, and create ourselves and our living as we imagine it to be, it will never be a clean beginning; it will be a creative process through which we download new data and a continuous balancing action of walking the fine line between the old and the new. To attain Self-Empowerment, you must embrace change and fight a powerful internal war between your illusions and reality. To change your actions, you must change your thoughts. To change your thoughts, you must change your beliefs. To change your beliefs, you must stop surviving in the stagnant data of your past and start creating a fresh new foundation for living in the dynamic ever-changing world of the present.

Consider this; why does a terrorist entertain thoughts of killing, while a Buddhist monk contemplates world peace? The answer is clear; your belief system serves as the mental factory from which your thoughts emerge. Negative beliefs based on illusions generate 'negative' thoughts that lead to negative results, and 'positive' beliefs based on the reality of feelings produce positive thoughts that lead to positive results.

You are the ultimate creator of how you live life's experiences and tests. To attain self-empowerment now, open your mind. Question your beliefs. Take personal responsibility, complete control and accountability for you own living and feelings. Throw out what's outdated and embrace what's new, exciting and real as you move through all the stages of cognition. Affirm the divine feelings for which you were born to this earth to affirm and live. But be aware, this is both liberating and totally scary.

Old man, what are the stages of cognition that you always refer to?

I will discuss this fact as we move along, but for the time being just realize that we have seven major experiences we pass through in our daily living.

1. Our physical desire for food and belonging
2. Our sexual desire for pleasure and procreation
3. Our internal confusion between right and wrong
4. Our Love in all its stages
5. Our Expression
6. Our intuitions
7. Our connection to God

But for now, to continue what we were discussing before, it is liberating when you understand that you are the ultimate creator of how your earthly living is being created. You will take full responsibility for your life resources. You make your own choices and decisions. You live according to your own personal beliefs and values. You are free from the anxiety of living up to the expectations of others. You experience the joy of being authentically yourself. But this living is frightening because You can no longer blame others for your failures and disappointments. You cannot cling to childish security from others. You must let go of the "old you," especially if that "old you" is holding you back.

So, the great secret to live a self-empowered life is to achieve physical, emotional, mental and spiritual empowerment as combined tools of awareness, expression and then action. Once you are aware of who you truly are, and that you are giving away your power through fear and blaming, you are more than halfway there. Express and balance your triangle of Power, Wisdom and Love to empower your actions.

Take a hard look at your life to see where you might be giving away your power. How are you letting other people define or control you or your behavior? Who are you blaming for your situation? What is your contribution to a conflict or life circumstance? What are you avoiding and what excuses are you giving yourself and others? What are your values of living? What feelings of illusion or reality you are affirming?

To examine yourself take small periods of time in your busy schedule, calm down and start meditating on your beliefs, your values and your actions. Sit in a quiet secluded place and contemplate the movie of your life in short films. Look at your films from a distance as an observer, but with a critic's eye. See where you enslaved yourself. See where you gave your power away. Observe your reactions and the outcomes of your reactions. Then as a Positive critic and a guide to yourself, see what steps could have been taken to produce a different outcome that would generate divine feelings of Courage instead of fear, Love instead of hate, Peace instead of turmoil and anger, Modesty instead of arrogance, Compassion instead of pity, Gratitude instead of need, freedom instead of slavery an most of all Reality instead of illusion.

Remove the Victim from every failure, heart break, fear, anger, anxiety you asserted yourself to be a victim. Stop self-sympathy to your self-made unhappy lonely life. Drop the victim, empower the Victor to be the essence of your life.

Drop your choking story. Stop being the leading character of your own misery. Take charge of your thinking. Let the old story fade away. Start developing the new person you choose to be. Form a new success story. Bend your Matrix. Develop a new air of Self-Empowerment. Create your living as the greatest expression of God's creation. Affirm the creative power of the divine being within you in every aspect of your existence. Regain our Power. View yourself as a creator, a designer of a new version of yourself. Take charge. Feel the grandest feeling of consciousness and let your energy flow.

Guidelines to Self-Empowerment

Repeat to yourself:

- I am in my peace regardless of the experience I will face.
- I am certain of my creative power regardless of whatever task I will do.
- I am humbly grateful for the opportunity to assert my divinity.
- I welcome the challenge to face life with the strength of my Creative Energy.
- My heart vibrates with kindness and love as one with every earthly creation.

CHAPTER THREE

THE MAGIC OF SELF-AWARENESS

Awareness is the most powerful means by which we can understand why we are on this earth. And Self-Awareness is the key to open the secrets gates of knowledge that shrouds our existence on this earth as humans. It clears our paths as we rediscover our purpose in occupying a fake physical form, thinking it is solid, belonging to the dust of the earth. But; until we are aware that we are all energy vibrating at different frequencies, producing our emotions and feelings as we move along in this time and space illusion, just to affirm our deity, we will always live the illusion that we are separate from the whole as single units trying to create a unique existence as humans, forgetting that our sole purpose is to affirm our unity in the trinity of life Power, Wisdom and Love. It is no more dust to dust; it is dust to heaven.

Could you please make it a bit simpler, a sweet voice came from the end of the room; I did not understand a word you said? What is awareness in general and how can we make it a simple study of the Self? What is this Dust to Heaven? I never heard it before.

I smiled and apologized as I recognized I was in my element talking to myself rather than teaching a class. I felt the hand of Maryam, my angel, the Queen of Heaven and the essence of love stroking the back of my hair calming me as she always did when I was a child. I glanced to where Suzanne, my partner, was sitting and saw her looking at me over her glasses as if saying as she always says: *You are not presenting a Ph.D. thesis Old Man, back to earth…*

I smiled as I looked at my student and said: My dear, living our conscious life is the greatest gift we are given as souls seeking the realm of the spirit. Though on one level or another we know that fact, we struggle in living our daily lives with much uncertainties, fears, worries, doubts and obligations leading us to confusion, depression, anxiety, loneliness, apathy and diminished self-worth. We start accepting situations in life, though self-destructing, as the way it is and the way it was destined for us. We lose the basic connection to our inner power and indulge into a life of living the status quo, afraid to rock the boat, aspiring an illusion of a physical security just to fulfill the illusion of our needs and wants even if it is to our demise. We become like the cat that licks an iron file, destroying its own tongue, just for the sake of tasting blood.

This same situation keeps repeating itself in many aspects of our lives, and in different stages of our daily living. We forget that we are on this earth simply to experience. We have the choice to feel any way we choose as we experience. But; we live as puppets in a marionette with no feelings except for what we have been programmed to perform and feel by the hands of the puppeteer. Through all this agony of self-slavery, we always have glimpses of self-grandeur and freedom; and the wooden puppet within us dreams of becoming Penoquio. We daydream and imagine what life could be. We hear voices banging in our heads of what could be, and what we could have done better to increase our lot in life; but we dismiss them as illusions, or we address them as it is God's will. We dismiss these voices as remote dreams unsuited to be part of our perception of what our lives are all about. We accept our lives as "this is the way it is meant to be", because God has chosen this life for us. We blame our miseries on God; then we become paralyzed, unable to change, afraid that we will upset God.

Then, when we try to do something about our lives, we are faced with self-doubts and major disappointments. We try to change; but the same feelings of detachment from the power that is needed to set us free, keep creeping up into our lives. We wonder why; why the same patterns keep following us in our lives? Why the same type of people keep creeping up in our reality? Why can't we change? Why can't we set ourselves free? Why can't we change the people we are with so we can find some happiness and self-actualization? And the preprogrammed answer keeps coming back to us. "We have tried, but it seems that regardless of what we do, we cannot do much. The reality of life is much stronger than our will to live the life we think should be ours". We look around and we see people living lives that we think we should have. We are scared numb to change. We envy others; we envy their houses, their cars, their money, their so-called freedom. We envy their spouses, and we wish for their way of living. We see their glamour and their so-called freedom, and we wish it belonged to us; thinking in our deepest selves that what they have is what we must have to become free.

Through all this turmoil, self-denial, confusion, self-destruction and emotional impotence, it becomes a matter of survival and absolute sanity to start having answers to our suffocating problems. So, we revert to our usual ways of solving our problems. We deal with life the way we were programmed to react. We invoke the same obsolete miserable patterns of solutions we are so used to leaning on. We manipulate our own thinking for the ineffectiveness of our solutions, convincing ourselves that if life was fair, we would be able to have what we desire. We blame the whole world for our demise, for the futility of our situations. We hate what we are in;

we hate our lives and we try to do better. But in doing so, we take the same package of self-pity, camouflage it with the idea of a fresh beginning, and apply it to a new approach. We rush to self-help books, read empowering articles, practice certain rituals, repeat memorized prayers, spin the prayer wheel, and rush to gurus that can save our lives; and to our surprise, we still wallow with our misery, and the first opportunity we are faced with what pushes our buttons, we revert back to what we memorized. We regress to anger, guilt, worry, doubt, hate, revenge, self-denial and a lot of self-made nonsense. Then the cycle begins again. We try to seek ourselves out of our stinking waste, so we perform the same acts of depending on others to solve our problems. We seek new self-help books, other ways of providing our miseries with solutions but to our surprise the outcome is still the same. We are still miserable, we hate ourselves, and we cannot find an easy way out. We cannot look beyond our noses; we hide behind our thumbs and swear that the sun does not shine. We fail to see our own power to solve any problem. Our inability to take charge of our lives is so ingrained deep in our sub-conscious minds, that whenever we try to advance in life we fail, simply because, we could swear by every sacred book, that the cause of our misery is always someone else, and thus someone else will solve our problems.

Here lies the crux of the problem. We blame life for our demise, while no entity in heaven or earth is the cause of our misery. It is US who are the cause of everything that happens in our lives, from birth to death and through everything in between. We are the cause of our problems, and we are the solutions. Every solution resides with us. We experience life the way we choose, and we create our own feelings the way we select. Whichever part of our Subconscious, Conscious or Super Conscious our mind acts upon, there manifests our realities. There begins our awareness; the total awareness of the body that supplies the experience, the mind that supplies the reality and the soul that supplies the motivation to experience. We all have the power and the means by which wisdom of self-empowerment is achieved. The trick to total awareness is to learn the power tools of choice by which we will understand the basics of liberating ourselves from the yoke of the so called "God's will" in our lives and start to take responsibility for what we create in life. The moment we master these tools, we will find our way to salvation and to empowerment. We will discover the power to create the grandest feeling of ourselves through the experience of our own created realities. The moment we reach this realization, we will reclaim our own powers from life and whomever we gave it to. Then, and only then, we can create our own solutions and accept life as we create it. At that time of ecstasy, what was anger will become disturbance of peace; what was fear will become a shortage in courage, what was worry will become an interruption of poise, what was doubt will become an intermission of certainty, and what was separation will become a break in totality.

Stay with me my friends, for soon we will dispel many illusions. We will learn how to reclaim our powers. We will become aware of the different bodies that make us humans. We will learn the great parts of manifesting the body, the mind and the soul and the awareness of each of these parts. Finally, we will learn all the necessary tools to deprogram our data banks and install new programs by which we can create our realities in this life the way we choose to. Then last, but not least, we will learn how to find the grandest part of ourselves regardless of what the experience might be...

So, settle down, allow your imagination to soar on the wings of the hawk, and let your realities tread this land with the heart of the wolf. Free you heart and prepare yourselves for a new beginning where you will become the focal point of your interest, and the creator of your happiness, majesty and greatness.

As you continue in understanding your Self Awareness, you will rediscover the reality of your inner beauty as you travel on this path of Self Awareness, enlightenment and healing as an outcome of your heart. You will understand life's purpose and meaning, to free your soul from its slavery to its obligations, fear, anger, worries, jealousy, greed, sorrow, guilt, self-pity, false pride and self-destruction. Read on, and focus your attention on your sole mission of being born; which is to assert your Divinity in creating the grandest vision of yourself, and reach the feelings of the divine soul of happiness, joy, peace, love, hope, serenity, humility, kindness, empathy, strength, truth, compassion and faith through the process of connecting your daily conscious awareness with your unconscious spiritual awareness which will ultimately lead them to Self-Awareness. Then you will remove the internal veils of doubt, letting the sparkle of your inner gem shine with your physical, emotional, mental and spiritual beauty. Soon if you choose to you will:

- Understand your life's purpose and meaning
- Connect with your living awareness
- Free yourself from fear, anger and worries
- Listen to your inner guidance and act upon it with confidence
- Connect with your spiritual awareness
- Manage stressful situations
- Eliminate negative habits
- Calm yourself before going into stressful situations
- Understand your living with obligation Vs. experiencing the process
- Break stubborn patterns that are blocking your full potential
- Become One with the Universal Energy. As it is outside it is inside.
- Become a Master of Your own universe.
- Understand it is not dust to dust, but dust to heaven. On earth as it is in heaven.

I do not understand your last sentence, all the holly books and all the priests say Dust to Dust, and now you are saying from Dust to Heaven; what do you mean by that? I am confused.

I smiled as I answered: We are in the lowest energy of our existence when we carry a physical body in this physical world. But, our aim in developing a physical low energy body in our mother's wombs, as we come from heaven (a higher vibrational energy) is to face all the lower energy experiences (Dust) and develop on an earthly plain (Dust) the grandest feeling (Heaven) regardless of the situation, experience or circumstance we are faced with. We do not come to earth to remain in dust, but to develop the grandest feelings we can achieve on this earth which is Heaven. In other words, earth which is dust is the place where we affirm heaven. Then when we die our bodies go back to Dust the basic physical energy of its chemical elements, and we go back to Heaven where we came from carrying back all the feelings we created on our earthly journey. Even if it sometimes feels like Hell, because we waste a whole life long on earth creating only Dust, dealing with dust and acknowledging only dust. We forget that we are on this earth only to experience Dust to heaven.

Do we all have the power to change dust to heaven? I have no power to take care of my daily affairs. How can I force myself to be in heaven all time as I live my life on this earth struggling to make ends meet, another student said?

I feel powerless, I cannot force the issue, and I do not have the strength to go on. How many times have you heard yourself or others say these words? But how many of you really understand what you are saying? So, let's explain briefly the difference between Power, force and Strength. My dear, I hear these statements all the time from my new students, clients and from others even those who academically can identify the difference between power and force in their physical jobs, they still fall short of identifying the difference between power and force when it comes to dealing with their emotions and reactions to events they face.

To briefly clarify this dilemma, we will say Power is the ability of the mind to think. It is the energy of the thought that you generate. While Force is putting this thought into action using logic and compassion to generate an emotion. The outcome of the force of emotions determines the strength of our reaction. The biggest difference between power and force is that power has no limitations, while force needs always to be justified. It is always your judgement of yourself that determines the power by which you react to what you face. In other words, thoughts hold power but create no emotion until you choose to act on the thought. The intensity of your judgement creates the force of your emotions and defines your outcome once you choose to act.

So, when you say I hate what is happening to me, all you are saying is you have no control over your outcome, and you have no power to change the experience you are facing. When you say I cannot force the issue, all you are truly saying is you have not used enough thought power to push your desired outcome to happen. But you are living the same result that happened before.

Your Life's Energy level, the God of creation within you, is what gives you the power to create your feelings. Your power level of creative vision in your daily living, as dust in your physical form, determines the strength of the Force which is needed to make things happen. The combination of both is what determines your level of consciousness or your spiritual growth (Heaven). Your spiritual growth determines the levels of thinking, feeling and acting you exhibit in your daily living. This level of your growth consciously determines your behavior, your actions and reactions; as you respond to any experience in life. Every decision you make is driven by your individual level of consciousness (Your Human Soul) where you create a matrix, or a special way of living. We either use your past programmed data of behaviors ready to be activated by your memories on how you dealt previously with conscious problems of living; or you use new levels of Life Energy from the Super Mind, the creative God or Higher Consciousness within us, to rise above our basic physical instincts, and gain the ability to force new desired decisions, feelings and every new action you take.

When you are faced with any stimulus or experience or situation that pushes your buttons you lose the power to create new outcomes. You rely on old solutions you always used before. That is why you feel stuck, upset, anxious unable to move ahead. In this moment of agony, you must stop immediately, take control of your mind and ask yourselves why are you doing the same things repeatedly? Why are you holding on? How can you force a new conclusion? To accomplish a new outcome, you must gain a new level of awareness. You must develop your thinking power to empower yourself to find peace and enforce a new solution.

I hope my dear I have briefly answered your question; we will discuss a lot of these subjects in our full sessions of Awareness, Expression and Empowerment.

I am really confused between when it comes to feelings and emotions, is there a difference between feelings and emotions? Why we are labeled as emotional not feelingal, a lady next to me said with a smile of her feelingal...

Of course, there is a big difference between feelings, emotions and moods though it is used interchangeably by many. Emotions are an instant reaction to a stimulus or to a situation or an event that we are faced with in our daily affairs. It is your way to survive by producing quick reactions to threats rewards and everything in between. They have been learned instant reactions coded and stored in your subconscious as data in a hard drive of a computer used to automatically respond to events you face. Emotions do not require thinking; they are an automatic response system to whatever you face in life. Emotions vary from one person to another depending on the program that each individual carry. Someone might see a spider and go into a frenzy, while someone else will let the spider crawl on their hand without any panic response. Some might faint out of fear if they see blood, while others like butchers deal with blood every day without having a reaction.

Feelings on the other hand are thoughts you choose to produce in response to different emotional stimuli. Feelings become a process you always use in your head as a guideline for your earthly being. Feelings guide you how to live, especially deciding what is right and what is wrong. Feelings dictate to you how to anticipate danger and how to prepare to face it, and how to insure long term survival of the physical and the spiritual. Your thoughts have a great impact on your feelings, and your feelings affect the way you behave, and your behavior is responsible for your results. Feelings are sparked by emotions and colored by thoughts, memories and images that are linked to certain emotions. While individual emotions are temporary, the feelings they cause can last for a lifetime. Emotions are common to all of us, and the feelings they produce are unique to every person. Feelings vary a lot from one person to another depending on your experiences and your individual stories and data that reside in your subconscious.

In summary your feelings are mental expressions and reactions to your emotions. They are colored by your personal experiences and beliefs. But regardless of how you feel, you can change your feelings depending on how you think and how you manage your emotions, and how you judge your experience.

Chapter Four

The Power tool
of Expression

As you are progressing in understanding the magic of self-awareness and living as Gods of Self-Creation in your daily physical life, it is time for me to introduce to you the grand tool of transforming the Magic of Awareness into a powerful tool of **Self-Expression** to create your true self in your daily living. I began addressing my assembled class as many gathered to continue the journey of discovering a new perspective of judgment as they express their daily living. Before I started my speech, a question from the back of the assembled class came rushing at me.

I am a mother of three rowdy kids that defy my ability to control. I think they have some power. They ask great questions and do not accept what I have been taught by my parents to tell them. I am really interested to know how you lived your own childhood to become who you are today, how did your parents deal with you? How can I help my children to overcome their doubts of god, church and life? A tear started to trickle down her cheek. Please help me.

I smiled with concern and said. Just bear with me my friend. Just develop the power within you first to be able to help yourself and then your children. Soon I will tell you the story of my own childhood and my own strife with all the questions within me. But then I had a great master teacher to guide my steps and sooth the fire within me. But until you become your own master to guide your own children, you will always be wandering why did you fail to guide them to find their own magic. So, stay with me my dear, for soon you will learn the art of expression that will change your life forever, and will empower you to guide your children to understand and manifest the creative power that they possess. All humans have the creative power within them to create the God of love, or the Devil of illusion. The choice of judgment is yours.

My dear friends this portion of this class is one of the important powerful landmarks on your journey to complete the mission for which you are born. It is the stage of living, if understood and acted upon will open the gate of the heart and allow the energy of life to consciously transfer the universal god of creation into the creative human. Contrary to many beliefs that require the Man to create Godhood by his physical deeds. In other words, learning the divine art of Self Expression will develop the power of God's Creation in you to modify your judgements as you affirm your grand feelings regardless of the experiences and tests you are facing or might face. Just remember, regardless of how your experiences may shape up, and your tests may present itself to be, you are a creative God, and your choice of powerful expressions will create the truth of your earthly existence as you may choose it to be.

And God said let there be light, and there was light. It is the expression of one's power of Thoughts, Passion and Love that makes life manifest. So, in this part of your journey you must release yourselves of your daily routine of thinking, and develop the art of expression within you to modify your self-designed Belief System that will stay with you to help you create outcomes and judgments as long as you live this earth and beyond. Shortly, you will modify the outcome of your expressions as you upgrade your Belief System until you can express the grandest feelings of the creative God within you, rather than expressing the reactive emotions of the human you think yourself to be.

Your mind's creations are arranged in the priority order and importance of all you believe and consent to as true, thus forming your expressions, or what you imagine yourself to be in every conscious moment of your earthly existence. What you express you become. What you judge you will feel. Your mind and your imagination will help you express and manifest any concept, idea, way, and belief you accept as truth about yourself. Your concept of yourself is all you consciously accept as true, and all you express reflects your concepts. It does not matter what gender you are, or what you do socially right or wrong, or what economic situation you are in, it is your mind that helps you express all the concepts of what you believe yourself to be, and your focused awareness will help you manifest it. Your level of expression determines your earthly state of being, and the quality of living you lead on this earthly planet. Thus, in this class it is vital that you start to express your desires and act upon your expressions by doing what matters to complete the mission for which you are born to fulfill.

This is a fascinating speech a lady next to me said, as her face turned red, but could you please say it in a simpler way.

I smiled at her and said: Self-expression is a bunch of values that include social toleration, life satisfaction, public expression and a desire for liberty. These individual values are always conflicted with judgments and survival values, different from one person to another across this world.

The Art of Self-Expression is the assertion or revealing of one's own individuality, such as individual traits, opinions, Judgments, personality, feelings, thoughts, or ideas, spirit, or character especially in speech, conversation, behavior, poetry or painting, writing, performing arts, music or dance. Self-expression is as vital to living as eating, drinking and breathing. It is how you interact with others and the world. It can be extremely fulfilling or irritably frustrating. Self-expression must be communicated to be fulfilled. It takes place through spoken communication, body language, and artwork and even your clothes and hairstyles. It includes how you express your feelings; decorate your homes and the way you drive a car.

Sometimes you do not even think about how you express your inner reality to those outside. It just happens automatically. At other times, you may strive to express something and disappointedly fall short of what you meant to get across. Many times, you are so confused to understand what you want to express. Other times, you have an idea of what you want to communicate, but you don't know how to make it clear. Sometimes you think you don't have the necessary skills or talents required to express yourselves.

Some of you have difficulty communicating because you are shy, insecure or just feel that your communication skills are lacking. You keep your mouths shut because you think that what you have to say will not make a difference anyway. There are times when your outer self-expression doesn't match our inner reality. You act nice and say superficially nice things when it is not how you feel. When you pretend to be or feel what you are not, you deny yourselves the enjoyment of who you really are.

Many of you think that you have to say, or feel, or be something other than what you are. You say things that you don't mean, thinking that it is what others want to hear. You pretend to feel things that seem acceptable so that others will approve of you. In this way you hide your true selves, both from others and your own selves. You bury your light in the darkness of pretense and 'trying to'. You express your wants, needs and desires in a certain way. However, as life brings you unexpected experiences, and your new situations demands new changes, is it reasonable to expect that the way you express yourselves remain the same?

Consider the parents of a child. As the child grows, the parents hopefully change the way they interact with the child as he or she matures. It is often easy for a parent to continue expressing themselves in the same way they have been used to. Yet a more mature child requires a more mature interaction with Mom and Dad.

My friends, how many times you felt that there is little you could say or do to contribute to a situation. How often have you thought that if you had a better personality, new skills or a different set of natural talents that your life would be better? How many times you have seen great talents and abilities in others around you and felt that they lack something important themselves. The truth is that the greatness you see in others is mirroring your own. Every situation in front of you can help you find confidence and courage to express yourself in whatever way it is natural to you. You may not always find out how much your input was valued by others, but you learn to trust that what you contribute is important. Just by being simply who you are, you can contribute to any situation in which you find yourself. Most humans have difficulty in clearly understanding what actions or expressions align with their critical nature and wish that someone else could tell them what is right for them.

My friends, you may be deeply influenced by concepts or ideals that others have created that don't really fit you. A huge inner conflict, and sometimes confusion, arises when you struggle to try to make yourself fit into them. But these concepts gently help turn you within to find the answers you seek. Stop running to others outside of the God within you for answers and support. Remove your own judgment of your own beliefs. Support your relationship with your inner self, and encourage trusting, valuing, loving and believing in yourself.

Sometimes your self-expression is repressed by your inability to accept your human mistakes and faults. The greatest deterrent to self-expression is the fear that others will not accept you. So, you believe your inability to find the self-acceptance that releases you from any fear of expressing yourself. When you find this acceptance within yourself, you will find it in others as well. Once you remove your fear of expressing yourself, imagine how free you can feel.

But I have been trying to change the way I feel, and I cannot. The hurt within me really suffocate me. I do not believe I have the power to really express my anger and guilt for allowing myself to be a victim of my decisions. The hurt within me is killing me. Please tell me how can express myself without hurting important people around me. A student fired at me.

My dear, I really understand what you are saying, but your internal hurt is an accumulation of your judgements that you chose to feel as you faced the experiences you met in your life. So, if you change your judgement of what has happened, and allow yourself the freedom to see what happened in a different view point, you will be able to express your bottled energy in an easier manner that will set you free.

This freedom helps you recognize the ways in which you judged yourselves and others, and the power of your self-expression. It shows you how you hide behind fake judgements. Once you peel off the layers of hypocrisy and nonsense, you can uncover who you really are. Freedom helps you find honesty, ease, and enthusiasm as you connect with your inner self.

Even if you know what you want to communicate, you may feel afraid to say what you want. Communication always has an element of risk. How will the other person or people receive what you are saying? Will they still love you when you express your true feelings? If you negotiate an issue with someone, will you lose face or risk your position? Will it mean that you'll have to give up or lose something? It supports you in taking the risk. When you do, you usually find that the other person reacts differently from how you feared they would. The essence helps you to know that there is only something to be gained and not lost through communication.

All forms of self-expression are risky when you fail to use the power of the Creative God within you. You do not know exactly how others will respond. Yet when you are willing to take a risk, you find that new levels of relationship can be achieved, problems can be solved, other perspectives can be found, and new ways of perceiving the world are open to you.

Self-expression can strengthen your ability to find what is appropriate. It helps you distribute your focus in all areas of your lives. It supports you in balancing and tempering your automatic responses. Sometimes, circumstances require you to adapt to conditions or situations in ways that you wouldn't under normal conditions. For instance, during some sort of crisis or difficult change you may accept things that you would not put up with during a more normal time of your lives. If you can exercise your ability to be acclimate to the situation, you may sometimes feel that it is easier to change your usual automatic response rather than feel awkward to fit a situation. It helps to adapt your self-expression to fit a situation with a clear vision of whether it is appropriate to do so.

Sometimes you may feel a deep inner impulse to express yourself, but you are unable to tap into your creative source that usually help you connect with your inner power. One of the biggest blocks to your expression is that you are not allowing your mind to accept a thought to become a possible outcome. Some of your great ideas start of as crazy ideas, but by allowing them the possibility of happening, they may grow into something usable. Often your mind may immediately shoot down a seemingly crazy idea by judging and analyzing it too soon. The Creativity Formula can help you stop from judging your ideas or yourself and thus blocking or stifling creativity.

Many times, you have a creative idea but are at a loss to know how to make it happen. Very often those of you who are easily inspired with ideas have difficulty finding how to secure them into practical result. This essence of expressing your God-self will help you with each step of making an idea manifest into reality. You can paint your life with the qualities you want to experience, or you can discover what you need to make a business plan become workable. Whatever the idea is, anchoring your Self Expression to your Logic, Passion and Love will help you become conscious of the step-by-step process to manifest it.

How many times have you found yourself in a new situation, convinced that you don't know how to handle it, only to find out that you did just fine by just being yourself? Learning and owning the following powerful formula is all the support you need to handle whatever situation you find yourself in.

The formula of Self-Expression is to believe and repeat the following:

I am the God I seek. I am one with God, and God is one with Me. There is no physical desire I want or seek, for the experience of the physical is only a test of my expressions.

At any moment in life you have yourself. Everything that you have experienced thus far in your life is the foundation for each successive judgement you make. If you find yourself in a challenging situation, you can apply the talent and skill that you successfully get yourself through. Express yourself with love and compassion. If you can view your capabilities from a wider perspective as an observer not as a victim, you will find that you are much more capable than you think. Repeating the formula of Self-Expression can help you see the bigger picture of yourself and own your level of self-mastery.

When you have confidence in yourself, you can always find what you need to handle any situation. By simply being present in the moment and using intuitive guidance with common sense, you can uncover levels of power that you might not have realized could be applied in a new way or different situation.

Though you get caught up in what is socially correct, Self-expression comes easiest when you affirm your God power to let go of your preconceived concepts and your familiar restrictions.

CHAPTER FIVE

THE REBELLION

As I watched the faces of the students looking at me, I felt the boy within me jumping out to speak. It was the time to finish today's class. So, I did dismiss the class to see them at the next session and sagged in my chair. The boy within me start recalling old memories of my life, how lucky that I am teaching today. How grateful I am for my teacher Steven the monk who put up with my arrogance, insecurities, fears and hate as young teenager confused, rebellious with hundreds of questions about God, life and living. I was afraid of death, hating the unfairness of The God that you must worship, and afraid of his retribution and revenge for insubordination. All what God said in his commandments to humans; love your parents, don't lust your neighbor's wife and cow, there is no God but me. I am the only one you must worship. It is a story like millions of stories that humans can relate to on this earth; struggling with internal confusion, and with old learned habits to deal with earthly uncertainties.

So, bear with me my friends as I tell you the story of my childhood confusion and rebellion with the help and love of an old monk, my teacher, friend and confident Steven. With Steven's guidance I moved on my path through the labors of life to reach the stage of internal belief, faith and control. I overcame my raging fire of uncertainties and created a soothing powerful energy within my own unique universe as a reflection of the universal energy of creation. My friends, I am telling you this story hoping that you will someday teach your children the truth about life and living, and the internal power to create their realities as they choose the experience.

As I relaxed my physical body in a beautiful state of self-hypnosis in a soothing meditative state, the Boy within me could not wait to take over. I could not understand that if God loved the world as the books claimed, and he created all living things, and all people are equal under God, why would he take up a sword and help one people over another? Why did God kill my grandfather, or did I kill him? Why would he choose one nation and call it his own while the rest of his creation could not receive just a drop of his mercy?

How can God be merciful and just when he did not create equal playing fields for all men and women to compete on? How can God be just when God gives two different lifestyles to a prince and a pauper, and expect the two of them to have the same experiences and the same understanding, and then demands the same equal worship and devotion from both? God gives humans wealth and power, and then he turns around and condemns them for having money and power. He tells them, "It is easier for a camel to enter through the eye of a needle than anyone of you to enter the kingdom of God" What kind of justice is this? What is this God? And where is God's kingdom? How can I pray to God and ask for help, when God is busy playing games with the lives of his creation enjoying killing them just for fun? Then, what about living? What about freedom? Why is the Bible all about death, sin, and devils, with some unclear visions of salvation? What is salvation? What is rebirth? Is my grandfather reborn? Is he living as an animal, bird, tree or a child? Or are the worms feasting on him forever? What is this incarnation nonsense? Why do priests and the books say that you will live forever either in heaven or in hell? Where can I find an answer to my dilemma? Did I kill my grandfather? Where is this God of mercy? All that the bible talks about is the fear of God, or else death is the result, and terrible roasting in hell is the end. But the funny thing that I could not understand is if death is the wage of sin as the bible claims, then why do sinners keep on living after death, not a luxury life, but being tormented forever in Hell? So, death is not the end? And when you die, you keep on living? So, my grandfather is living!!! If he is so, why can't I talk to him? I want him to tell me if I really killed him. Why does the bible not tell us what really happens when you die and are not being roasted in hell? Where do you go? Why no one can tell me the answer in a plain language that I can understand instead of being shrouded with mystery and in stories that could not be deciphered? And then if God is fair and just, how can this great God decide that two people are good or bad when the two persons are not given the same experience in life? How can God judge fairly between them? Did I kill my grandfather? Did my uncle kill my grandfather? Did god kill my grandfather? Or was it my grandfather's time to die regardless of what I did or did not do?

I asked my teachers. I asked my parents. I asked my priests, but no one could give me an intelligent definite answer. All their answers were: "Maybe... No one came back from death to tell us... Just have faith. Follow what the bible tells you... Do not ask such questions; it is sacrilege to think in this way...; "Never mention the name of god in this way, you are his slave, and the head of wisdom is to fear god". But the more I heard these answers the stronger my resolve became to find an answer. I became a rebel. I fought for the heck of fighting and disagreed for the enjoyment of disagreeing. I said no to everything just for the heck of saying no. My friends and I made a small untouchable gang at school and created havoc for teachers. I rebelled against authority and anything that resembled rules and regulation because it reminded me of the unjust rules of the murderous God who used my childhood innocence, and my uncle's rage to kill my grandfather. But, in the depth of my heart, I knew my turmoil must stop. I knew that somewhere in this vast universe, there must be an answer.

Then one evening as I lay down on my bed listening to the music of raindrops softly drumming on my bedroom's window and watching the dying sun rays trying to penetrate the thinning clouds, I lost touch with reality. I went into a trance between sleep and awakening. I felt my breathing slowly regulating itself to the beat of the rain. My eyes half opened not able to close. My face relaxed. My Jaw dropped. My muscles relaxed. I felt soothing warmth flowing from my head down my spine to the tips of my toes. I lost control of my senses. I could not move a muscle as if my whole body did not belong to me. I could not feel anything around me. My limbs were numb, I could not move. I felt no pain. I could not think. What is happening to me? I wanted to sit up, but I could not find my body. My heart was racing. My mouth was dry. I could not find my tongue to call for help.

"Mother Mary please hold me". The light in my room became brighter. Why and how can I see myself lying in bed? Fear crept into my essence. Am I dead? No, No, No I cannot die… Where is this awful music coming from? It is the sound of that horrible funeral procession down the street. Are they coming for me? I felt a jolt as the huge drum sounded its miserable tune. My head spun with pain. My body was full of cold sweat. My heart almost stopped. I could feel my arms, and legs. I could feel my tongue licking my dry lips. My whole body trembled. I pushed myself into the fetus position. I tasted my salty tears as they trickled down my cheeks into the corner of my mouth. What happened to me? Is this another bad dream? Did I really see my body lying down? Did I really float above my body? Or was this another one of those dreams that haunt my being? I cannot think for myself. Someone must tell me.

I cannot tell my parents; they will dismiss me as usual by making me repeat ten Hail Mary's for everyone Our Father… I cannot talk to priests, they already dismissed me as a no-good delusional boy who thinks that churches are Ali Baba's cave and the priests are worse than the forty thieves. Where can I go? Whom can I talk to? I want to understand. I want the truth. I have a million questions rattling in my brain like a pinball machine ready to Tilt... Then to add to my confusion I saw myself from above lying in my bed... How can I say this had happened to me and to whom can I say it? Where is this God forsaken guide, the teacher that the soothing voice in my dreams always promised that he/ she/ or it will soon appear, and I will see? I guess (soon) to this voice, is quite different than the soon I am used to.

I went back to my Bible seeking the answers, but my Bible is confusing; it has more riddles than answers. The story of creation, Adam and Eve, the Flood, the confusing identity of God... Then what is this idiocy about the Original Sin? What is this vengeful jealous and sadistic confused egotistic God that gives the people a free will, and then he destroys the world just because his creation gained knowledge? Why do you have to experience every aspect of life if you are not supposed to gain knowledge? Then how does God claim that all human creations are equal underneath the sun when a female is made a subordinate and a servant to man? Then if a man is better and superior to a woman, how could a woman, a lesser human, convince him to defy God? Why would a master listen to a servant? What is this God that you have to believe in, that chooses a group of his human creation over another and calls them his own; then he uses his powers of pestilence, fire, and misery as a sword to massacre whole nations just because they do not agree with his chosen people? Then, and with the same logic, is it justifiable for all the tyrants and murderers that passed through the history of the earth to claim themselves as a superior race and to eliminated the so called inferior nations and other nations upon nations just because the God of the Bible did so himself? Why is the God of Creation completely different from the God of the New Testament? One is an obnoxious, jealous, egotistic murderer, and the second is the God of love, understanding and compassion? How many Gods are there? Does

God suffer from multiple personalities and identities, or are there many Gods not only a single creator? What is the truth? Why only small portions of the teachings of Jesus were kept? What happened to all his teachings? Then who is the true disciple Paul or Peter? Which church tells the truth? If the truth is one, and its source is one, then why do you have all these religions, churches, temples, mosques and so on, and everyone claims to be the truth? Oh God please attend to me... I am lost.

Days have passed, and few years rolled on and I could not find answers to my lingering questions. I read the world's holy books, but I could not understand. I was 15 years old full of questions but as ignorant and confused as I could be. I investigated ancient Greece and the Gods of Olympus for answers, but I found no definite answers. I studied translations of the ancient Sumerian civilization written in the Cuneiform language to no avail, but for more confusion as I saw pictures of aliens in space ships carved in stones being referred to as Gods, and all the stories of creation that I was told by the priest, my teachers and my parents, were all false according to the Sumerian Epic of Creation. I searched the pyramids and the ancient religions of Egypt for answers, but as I tried to understand the ancient religions of Osiris Isis and Horus doubt filled my heart and I could not proceed. I tried to learn the Kabala but still I could not understand the truth behind the tree of life. I read the Upanishads Veda, but it was much deeper than I could dive into. I spoke with the Sufis; I read the volumes of Rumi but again I could not find my answers. I read Socrates, Pythagoras, Nietzsche, Gibran and many other philosophers, historians and religious gurus. In all that I have read, I could catch a glimpse of an understanding deeper than the written words; but as soon as I found that line for knowledge, I would lose it with a confused mind grasping for every straw of every book I could read.

What is it then? Why can't I understand? Why so much knowledge, and why so much confusion? Why is all this knowledge shrouded with masks and veils? Why isn't it a straightforward talk? And why is it left to individuals to interpret and decipher all that is written, everyone as he individually pleases? I carried all this confusion in my heart. My mind swam in the mud pits of uncertainties to the point of apathy, to the point of rebellion; an up rise against all social and religious values and traditions grew in my heart. Nothing mattered any more. No man-made idealism had any value anymore. No god nor devil, no angel nor demon. My dreams kept haunting me, but they did not matter anymore. I stopped searching for my guide. I even forgot that I was promised that my guide would soon appear and then I will see.

Ready or not, I did not care anymore. But through all the facade of toughness and rebellion, a tender voice kept whispering in my ears. It came to me on nights of peace as I secluded myself with the stars under my favorite tree at the slope of a beautiful mountain overseeing heaven and earth. I was almost 16 years old when on a camping trip, and as I sat alone with my thoughts; I wondered if the stars are made for our enjoyment, or there might be other civilizations occupying these stars and planets; and maybe some lonely person like me is looking towards heaven at our earth from his favorite spot on that star and wondering if you humans ever exist. My thoughts of care flew so far that I did not hear the light steps bending the dry grass near me. Suddenly with a jolt to my head, my instinct of survival pushed my soaring thoughts back into my head and I jumped into attention. I looked to my side ready to fight or run away according to what I would face in front of me; when to my surprise I saw the most beautiful genuine smile I have ever seen in my life grinning from underneath a massive blob of hair attached to a man's face. I saw wide eyes glittering with tenderness, and a forehead half covered with a brown monk's hood attached to a brown robe covering his body to the tips of the toes. I knew this man. He was the one I made fun of when he was preparing the evening mass as we all gathered on this beautiful night of August in summer camp. *"I am sorry I startled you,"* he said as he asked me to sit down. His eyes fixed into mine and the smile never departed his lips. I could not move but to sit down. I stared into his face and felt comfort. His glowing face soothed my startled fears, and his voice reminded me of the tender calm voice I used to hear in my dreams. I was overtaken by a hidden power of calmness and ease. I could not find my tongue. I pretended to compose myself, and with a smirk of uncertainty on my face, which I am well famous for, I started to apologize for my behavior this evening before mass, when He gently raised his hand towards me and with two fingers he touched my lips and said: *"Shhhhh… No need for apology, what came out of you is the residue of a troubled heart and an explosion of a volcano boiling under the pressures of many years of uncertainties"*. My eyes opened wide. My chin dropped, and my lips parted with surprise. "Aren't you mad at me," I said, after all what I have done to you this evening? He said with a tender voice trying to hide a chuckle: *"No I am not; I am sorry I could not measure up to your standards for humanity. My name is Steven I am a monk, he said, and I surely know who you are. Your temper and restlessness are well known throughout this camp"*. I looked straight into his eyes as I felt my tears starting to develop in my eyes. "I am really sorry," I said. "I cannot bring myself to accept this fake ritual of a mass to a God that does not care beyond the realm of his own ego and demands subordination without questioning. No wonder Alexander the Great, Genkis Khan, the Roman Emperors, the Catholic Popes, Napoleon, Hitler, and every person who wanted to conquer and subjugate the world tried to imitate him". He noticed the quiver in my voice and said without hesitation: *"You are right. If God is all this, then there is no use in following him. Humanity must find another God to follow"*. I was stunned with surprise. His words covered my wounded heart with a healing balsam, and his soothing smile penetrated the depth of my spirit to subdue my raging volcano. I covered my face with my palms as my tears poured down my face. For once in my life a priest agreed with me. He did not condemn me as a heretic and damned my soul to eternal fire, but he accepted me as an equal, and embraced my attacking ignorance with a smile of love and understanding. He stretched his arms and embraced me. My head fell on his shoulder and I sobbed for minutes that felt like eternity. I knew then that my search was over. I have found my promised teacher, an old friar on the slope of the mountain underneath my favorite tree. Yet, I have not discovered the sight I was promised to see.

"I have waited for you so many years, are you the promised teacher whom that little voice that soothed my dreams throughout most of my childhood promised me will appear"? Please tell me I said as I stared in this man's eyes. Are you really this teacher that will sooth my raging confusion, and open the gates of heaven in front of me? I have a million questions, "I said", I am so confused. Please let me now. Please explain to me. Did my grandfather die because of me? Did my words kill my grandfather? Did my lie cause my grandfather's death? I cannot bare this pressure anymore; I have been living with this nightmare all my life. My life has been a dream after a confusing dream all mingled with reality. My understanding of life is nothing but a question following a question with no answers. I am afraid of death. Am I a murderer? I do not understand. Why all this confusion? Why all this uncertainty? Why all this interwoven jungle of religion? Why, why, and why???

My teacher stretched his hand and with two fingers on my lips he bid me to stop. *"I know you have a million questions to ask. I know you are confused. But first things first my Teacher said, did you eat?"* My temper almost flared. I am asking you about all my life's confusion, and all you care about now is food! A smile appeared on his lips, and he laughed so hard that his stomach started to bounce. *"I cannot have so much fun at this old age, my teacher said, you are killing me"*. I felt awkward and embarrassed. Is he for real? My thoughts bounced around my brain while my mouth kept shut, or is he an old fool who is trying to make fun of me? I did not know what to think. Then mercifully he said:

"Just let it go. Let it be for now. The first rule of understanding is to calm down, and to disengage yourself from the source of your confusion; while keeping the question in mind as your focal point, you must learn to see it from a distance. You will be surprised how close you are to the answer. It is usually too close to your face and that is why you cannot see it. Just disengage yourself from your problem and look at it as a spectator and you will easily see the answer. If you have a small cut or a rash on your face, and it is itching and bothering you a lot, you will not be able to identify what is on your face unless you use a mirror to see yourself, or ask a friend to check it out for you."

How can I do that, I said, which mirror do I use to see the reflection of my soul? I have asked many friends and many teachers. I got nothing but a confused answer from all of them; so, by God, what are you talking about. I have lived all my life searching for answers to many questions, guilt and fear. Whenever I thought I got a glimpse of an answer, many questions come flooding into my brain. I then try to answer the new questions, which make me lose track of what the original question was. My face was starting to get hot. The vein in my left temple, the sign of my volcano starting to erupt, bulged and my voice pitch was rising.

But my teacher had no reaction; he sat down watching me as if in a daze. I focused my eyes on him, and my rage subsided. I became mesmerized by his smile and self-confidence. I could see the depth of the universe in his eyes and I could feel the sense of my littleness is his tender smile. I stopped talking afraid that my insignificant rattling would disturb this serene calmness that projected from this god-sent monk towards me. I froze with a sense of calmness that overcame my being. What is happening to me? I whispered in my mind, afraid to raise the pitch of my question so that I would not disturb my teacher. Where did this calmness come from? His tender eyes are penetrating my soul. I feel at ease; nothing seems to matter anymore. Then to my relief my teacher broke the silence and said: *"Before you can understand life and all its mysteries you have to understand living.*

You have to understand yourself; and before you can analyze God and man you have to analyze yourself, and to analyze yourself you have to learn how to just let it go". What do you mean by all this, I said? Then out of the blue my teacher said: *"Did you eat my son? I am hungry. Why don't you go and grab couple of sandwiches from the dinner table and you will continue after you eat"?* A smirk appeared on my face, and the little devil in me started to say: no wonder monks are fat and funny, all what they think about is eating. As if he was reading my thoughts, my teacher said: *"If we do not take care of this body, we will lose the only vehicle available for us to experience this world, and then we would lose a valuable chance to experience the fire of our existence".* But for now, Just Let It Go… Just Let It Be…

CHAPTER SIX

THE SECRET OF LETTING GO.

Do not ask me why you cannot let go; simply ask yourself why you are still holding on.
— **Suhail S. Jarroush**

It is a new day, and a new session with my beloved students. I dosed off while meditating a bit before the class started, and my thoughts flew to the edge of my divine soul. How often have you heard people telling you to just let go? How many times you shook your heads and said: "I wish I can. I am so angry. It is so difficult. It really hurts deep. I cannot take it anymore. If you were in my shoes you will do the same." How many times you had to swallow your tears and feel the lumps in your throats. How many times you had to do what you have to do because it is your obligation, and it is the right thing to do, regardless of how hurt you felt, and regardless of how miserable you became. "It is the right thing to do. My mom did it. My father did it. This is how I was brought up. God wants it so. I cannot do anything about it. This is my destiny- ".

"How stupid is my life. I cannot take it anymore. I am going to explode. I cannot understand this confusion within me". I fired this barrage of words at Steven as he came into my view. I was barely 16 and my head and heart

were full of turmoil, sadness, bitterness. I hated every organized religion where God has nothing else to do in life but wait for you to sin so that he will punish you with eternal fire. I hated the school system where the convincing force of communication was a punishment just because you dared to defy the authority and asked why. I was confused in a family system where no one explained to you how and why you have to do what you are told, but just do it simply because they said so, and God forbid if you dare to defy this authority, the head of the house hold the father and the mother, acting by authority from God will make your life so miserable especially if you live in a socially rigid patriarchal society where children and women were second class citizens. I looked at my guide aching for an answer hoping to receive some relief for my chocking anger. All I got from him was a wide peaceful smile as he muttered his famous words *"Just let it go"*. Nothing irritated me more than these infamous words uttered by this monk, *Just Let It go*... How the F#@k can I let it go when it is stuck in my throat choking me to death?

But, as I moved through time, and now I have my own students and friends, clients and patients asking me similar questions; I find myself acting as my guide once did flashing my own smile, uttering the same infamous words *"Just let it go"*, and to my amusement I hear the same answer I used to fire long time ago, *"How the –Bleep- can I do that?"*.

I came back to my senses after seconds that felt like eternity. I motioned to my student to sit and listen, for soon she will understand.

I came back to my senses as the class started. I heard two mates talking as they walked in:

"How the –Bleep- can I do that, how the F#@k can I let go?" I smiled at them. I have heard this question so many times, and each time I hear it, I remember Steven's smile soothing my temperament as I asked my questions.

To answer this question, we must begin by understanding simple basic rules of life and living. We must really dig deep within us to the core of our existence. We must reveal the simple basic truth that shines within us. We must tear the veils of ignorance that separate us from our deepest self. We must drop the masks behind which we hide our true thoughts, feelings and emotions. We must stand naked beneath the shower of our own true light bathing in the sun of our own glory. What a magnificent thought to be out in the world to be free. Free of our own problems, sadness, worries, anger, guilt, jealousy and the list go on... Free of devastating circumstances, and of the sticks in our wheels. Free of a pre-destined life where God, our parents, our religion, our school, our circumstances, our friends, our spouse, our needs and wants define who we are, how we live, how we feel, how we think, how we act, how we perform and how we see ourselves.

"But It is very difficult to even think that I could be free", another student fired from across the room as she was attending the Spiritual Awakening course that I run twice a year. *"I have been married for over twenty-five years. My job in life is to make my husband happy and to attend to my children's need. I do not have time for myself. My husband demands that his food be prepared, he demands that his sexual needs be satisfied and he demands that I must be at his service anytime he beckons, or else he explodes into a bout of anger that frightens the daylight out of me and shakes my existence to the bottom pit of my stomach. I hate my life, tears run down my face when I am alone. I do not dare to cry in front of him, or he will explode in his usual bout of anger, and he might leave the house for a day or two leaving me alone with the children. This is my destiny; I must accept my demise so that I will keep peace at home for the sake of my children. Maybe I am a bad wife, a bad mother, and a bad person as my husband labels me. It is my fault that my husband explodes with this rage, breaking furniture and putting his fist through walls. I am a bad person that deserves to be treated this way, and I deserve to be punished. I am here to find the truth. Am I this*

terrible person that deserves all this misery? What have I done wrong to God to deserve this punishment"?

Her tears ran down her cheeks as she looked at me with helpless eyes searching my eyes for an answer. Silence moved over the heads of the students in the class. Some shook their heads in disbelief, some were sharing the student her tears recalling their own miseries, but they all looked at me for an answer as my lips broke out in my usual smile as I said: "Why are you holding on to it; just let it go, just let it be. Soon you will remember the power that is within you, the power of God that resides within your mind, heart and throat. Bear with me my dear, soon you will find your answer. Just listen to me for now, open your heart, clear your mind and only for this moment, let go of all your problems. Refocus your mind just for this moment on something other than your pain. Focus your eyes in my eyes regardless of how I move and let nothing but my ugly face (I said this with a grin) become real for you at this moment. Focus your mind on a single thought; it is the freedom of your expression and the liberation of your heart. Feel nothing but your own shallow breath filling your lungs with a new hope and engulfing your heart with confidence courage and self-control. Breathe in slowly and breathe out with a mighty blow of air sending all your bottled emotions away from you. Great... do that again. Just live this moment, enjoy your being in this class and for a moment in time just live your freedoms as you choose it to be". She stared at me with eyes of hope; and as I cracked a smile, I noticed through her fingers as she wiped her tears a tiny grin tickling her lips. She looked me straight in the eyes. She gave out a long sigh and her tiny grin became a smile of hope and peace.

You have done nothing wrong my dear. It is not a punishment. It is not an act of revenge from God. God is not human. God is a spirit, and the spirit does not have an ego to bruise. God is not he, she or it. God is all that was, is and will ever be. God does not wield the sword of misery in your face and lay you down as a doormat in your own home to revenge his bruised honor that is tainted by your sin. Only human beings, who are dominated by their physical instinct of survival, or the animals in their kingdom at a lower scale of evolution, feel the need to dominate the physical existence, and feel the need to avenge the bruises of the ego. Calm down, listen to me my dear (I put my hands around my mouth in a joking manner as if to stop anyone else present from hearing what I am about to say, but said it in a loud voice) I am going to reveal to you a small secret. There is no sin against God, you only sin against yourself. (I looked her straight in the eyes as I saw her jaw drops) There is no physical place called hell, and there is no physical eternal fire where you will burn for eternity. There is no eternal damnation no accusation, prosecution, judgment and no execution. There are no sins in life; there are only experiences in living through which you produce a wide range of feelings; some feelings will lift us to the apex of euphoria, and other feelings will drag us into the dark pit of misery. It is no one's power over you that make you do what you do not want to be done, and produce what you do not want to feel; it is you and you alone that decide the ways, conditions, emotions and feelings by which your life would be run.

Through your fears and programmed beliefs, you create many emotions that affect your perceptions of reality and create your own truths. The way you look at problems in your life will assert them to be problems that choke your existence or will change problems into experiences that you can handle and let go. The moment you believe that you can create any reality you choose by living a life of your own choice, you will define your reality towards every experience you face as you travel through the pathway of time. You become your own accuser, prosecutor, judge and executioner or you will become you own champion, rescuer, redeemer and savior. You will become your own master with powers to create your own heaven or your own hell. You will be able to consciously create your life, to draw on the experiences you choose, and then define your reality towards these experiences. You will have the freedom to accept these experiences, reject

WHAT WOULD THIS OLD MAN SAY

them and change them the way you desire. But the greatest sin you commit against yourself is by constantly refusing to acknowledge the fact that you have the total power within you to change your misery into euphoria, and your hell into heaven.

It is ok, you have my permission, if you need permission from anyone, to change the course of your life, to balance your thinking, your feelings and your actions and acknowledge the great love of God traveling through your being. There is no sin other than thinking that there is a disconnection and a deep gap between you and God. There is no greater fallacy and no greater an illusion than your need to bridge that gap by suffering. God is the source of all love that permeates consciousness. God does not enjoy your suffering nor cause you to suffer. God does not take pleasure in your misery nor causes you to be miserable. You create your own misery, you create your own suffering, and you create your own hell, not God.

So why can't I let go? Why do I live in my misery? If I am all that you have just told me, why can't I feel the power of God within me? Then are you for real? Do you expect me to believe that God and I are one? Do you really want me to believe that there is no heaven or hell, there is no judgment and there is no sin and eternal fire? You are scaring the daylight out of me...How can you say that I am the source of my own misery? I am tired, I feel empty, I am busting my rear end to please my husband and my kids, my family, and to be all I can to everyone around me without asking anything in return, are you saying this is not my obligation to them? Are you telling me that I Am the source of my emptiness? Why would I chose this life of misery? I do not understand I am confused, what the heck are you saying?

I stood motionless in the middle of the class. For a moment the vision of my youth came rushing down my memory lane. Wasn't it but only a few years ago when I rattled all these questions to Steven my guide? All I could see in this moment, manifesting in front of me, was Steven's beautiful smile assuring me to bring forth the trail of words that jammed my throat. I felt myself beyond my body as the words tried to race past my lips. I stood in silence but for few seconds that felt like a lifetime. I felt the hand of God moving across my forehead and the voice in my head saying, "It is time my son. It is time to reveal what I have been teaching you. For years I have calmed you down to sleep, but now I am calming you down to reveal the truth. Do not doubt yourself; I am with you through eternity".

I broke the deadly silence in class with my famous smile flowing from the depth of my heart, which brought soothing calmness into the hearts of my students. I started firing through my vocal voice downloads of information running through my mind. And as if through the tongue of my teacher I started to say: "It is not enough to say why I cannot let go of all my thoughts, fears, guilt, worry, anger, behaviors, patterns and addictions. It is time to start asking yourself why you hold on to these fears' patterns and addictions. When you ask why I cannot let go, you give your fears the power to determine your feelings and your conscious life. You enslave yourself to your own belief system of hopelessness and weakness with a caged inability to be free, simply pleading with your miseries to ease up on you so that you will have some breathing room. But the moment you give yourself permission to ask yourself with a loud voice, why are you holding on to your devastating pains, you will give yourself the boost and the solid ground from which you can start to evaluate your belief system that keeps you chained to your beliefs, addictions and behaviors. You will start to think of a much more powerful attitude of looking at yourself from a different angle with a new perspective that will change your perception of yourself. You will start to create a new pattern of thinking that will produce new feelings and new ways by which you can see yourself.

"But how can I control my feelings? I feel like a soda can, the moment someone shakes me, I explode with anger. And if I do not explode, because I am

taught it is not socially polite to do so, I keep this anger within me, and I feel anxiety eating in me till my tears start to flow. I start blaming myself for all that happened. And now I hear you tell me I can control all this as if I am a magician. Are you a magician? If you are a magician and you have a magic wand, please wave it and relieve my agony Another student fired from across the room with a chuckle of sarcasm in her voice *"Yea Merlin move your wand over our heads and save us all from looking at ourselves".*

'The magic is yours my dear, I answered with compassion and empathy. You are the magician. But you are turning your own magic against you. You are destroying yourself by the power of your own magic. You automatically pull old obsolete magic from your old magic bag that you have applied before in different situations and apply them to new experiences. So, you react to events and situations that face you in every moment of your conscious life as you have quickly reacted before without a second thought of acting differently. This automatic old reaction to new experiences will produce old obsolete feelings to new events that require a new set of emotions, feelings and actions. So the more you use your automatic responses in everyday living rather than using new thinking, you will bring old feelings of fear, hate, anger, guilt, helplessness and enslavement that you felt before at different stages of your age even as a child, or even in past lives into new events. You will now automatically and without knowing how or why suddenly feel sad, fearful, angry and guilty, feeling totally lost and so down and confused. When you react with anger to something you do not like, just be aware that it is you that is making yourself angry not the thing that you are angry about. Someone or some situation may push your buttons, but you, automatically and without understanding why, will allow your emotions to flair, your veins start to pop up, your heart starts to race, your voice pitch rises. You will start to react, (or act the same way you have acted before) to protect your ego, your human soul, from the feelings of belittlement. Thus, you will create feelings of anger, and the outcome of anger, traps you in a state of anger. So, remember my dear friend, if you did not create your buttons by turning the power of your magic against yourself, no one could push them. The moment you create buttons, your buttons will be pushed.

But think now, if you have God's power to create a belief system with infinite buttons to be pushed and the capacity to make yourself angry, you can use the same power to change your belief system to eliminate your buttons, and the capacity to make yourself happy. The difference in both situations is that you automatically, unconsciously make yourself angry; but you are not aware that you have the same power and capacity to consciously create whatever feeling and state of being you choose to create. The same power and magic that creates anger and distress can create happiness and peace. The key is for you to take control of this magic consciously.

Are you joking with me? If I have such a great power, why am I sitting in your Self Discovery class to learn how to let go?

One of the students asked with a smirk, of "I got you", on her face.

I scanned the faces of my students and saw a steady grip of uncertainty printed on their faces. I felt the wheels of their thoughts spinning fast, but like a hamster running on a spinning wheel going nowhere.

Then after a moment of deadly silence that felt like eternity, I felt the hand of Maryam running through the back of my hair and I said: You are right my dear lady in doubting your power, because as of yet, you have no concept of who you are. You are not aware of your own power to create any feeling you choose. You automatically react to life's situations without knowing why you do what you do. And when you calm down, you will start questioning yourself (Why did I do what I have done? Why did I accept this bull crap? I should have acted in a different way, I should have done so and so….) and as you question yourself, you will end up feeling guilty for doing what you did, and you start acting like a victim who has been wronged by life and its circumstances. You will allow anger, sadness, doubt, worry, fear and stress to dominate your life. Your only way out of your choking feelings is to resort to tears, dry mouth, stomach cramps, headaches, anxiety and depression to relieve your emotions.

But there is no need to do all that. As you automatically create your demise, you have the same capacity to purposely create your glory and any other feeling you choose to have, when you become aware that this power is born with you at the moment of your conception. It is your birthright. Remember that you are born in the image of God, a creator in the energy of a creator, with the capacity to create whatever you choose to create, from your demise to the grandest feelings of the divine soul.

So, knowing that you have the power to create whatever feeling you choose to have on this earth within any experience you face, then why do you hold on to your judgments, feelings and emotions, towards the experience, rather than Just letting it go. I said with authority guiding my class to focus on their own experiences.

"But that sounds the same. It seems like a riddle that has no answer" another student fired at me from her comfortable seat on the floor. *"Are we going to study psychology or the power of life?"*

I smiled at her quick reaction to what I said, and I enjoyed her enthusiasm in expressing herself. I looked at her with compassion and remembering my fiery questions to Steven and recalling his tender smile as he used to touch my forehead with a tender nudge of love and say "Think my little wandering hawk, a name Steven used to always call me by, think of what you are saying. Do not fire your words with pure emotion but create a balance between your thoughts and expressions and I promise you that your words will someday create wonders". These words passed through my insight as my student fired her emotional question at me. I felt the tender nudge of Steven's hand on my forehead as I answered my student: "Your enthusiasm in asking your question is the same enthusiasm needed to understand what I have said. Please allow your fiery energy to open a path of understanding through your emotions, rather than forming a solid energy block that prevents you from accepting any explanations I am sending towards you. Your question to me is a great example of the difference of why you cannot let go, and why you hold on to your beliefs. Recognizing the feelings that ignited your question will help you determine if you are holding on to your belief systems or if you are unable to let go. In other words, if you ask a question to understand why you have a solid grip on your feelings, you will give yourself the power to learn new tools that will help you release your grip, change and let go. But if you fire an emotional question to merely assert the power of your belief system, then there is no tool that you can learn that will help you change. Your belief system will become your master, and regardless of how much you try, you cannot let go because the power to change is not yours anymore, but it belongs to your belief system".

So my friend, start understanding this belief system that enslaves you, controls your actions and jails you in your patterns and addictions, or simply switch to a new belief system that you control and you change as you please, giving you the power to act as you please.

"But what is the difference between our belief system and us? Aren't we the same? Aren't we the product of our own beliefs?"

Of course, we become the product of our beliefs. We allow our deeply programmed beliefs dominate our lives; we will react to life's experiences in the same manner as we previously did produce the same result as we generated before. These reactions trap us in our patterns, behaviors and addictions wondering why we cannot let go of our fear, guilt, demise, worry, anger and so many other feelings that choke our lives. But the moment we start asking why we are holding on to our patterns, behaviors and addictions, we start our conscious process to release the grip of our belief systems on our daily actions. This freedom to choose will allow us to open ourselves to new ideas, ways and tools that will help us change our beliefs thus changing our outcomes in our conscious daily living.

I looked at my students all frozen in their seats with their thoughts resting on top of their heads like a heavy cloud. I could hear a pin if it dropped on the carpeted floor. They were looking at me with anticipation of that magic formula that will change their lives forever. I posed for a moment then I flashed my smile and said "wake up guys; it's not time to rest now. This is the time to work. You will have enough time to contemplate later. Do you want a fish to satisfy your present hunger I asked, or do you want to learn how to fish, so that you will never be hungry again? (I liberally borrowed this question from my dearest friend, Jesus the Nazarene). I flashed my smile scanning my students' faces. "If you want a fish please see me in my office after class, and I will give you a temporary fix. But, if you choose to learn how to fish and never go hungry again, then listen to me. It is time you become aware of your own magical power. Let us try to figure out who you are and what is that belief system and how it is found? What gives this system the power over our lives? So, let us start from the beginning. Let us start with the ABC's of Life and Living".

I turned back to locate my seat. I heard a sigh of relief coming from a corner of the class. I grinned as I leaned back in my chair feeling the hands of Maryam running over my forehead and the back of my neck, while listening to the voices of my friends (my spiritual guides) dashing through my mind. I felt a calmness and deep tingling sensation of love encircling my body. I felt the hands of Steven and my other guides resting on my shoulders assuring me to go on. A tear of joy started to form in the corner of my eyes, and I felt it trickling down my cheeks. I leaned my head backwards till I was able to catch my breath, then with calmness of the ages I said: Let us start from the beginning.

CHAPTER SEVEN

WHO ARE YOU?

You are not what you see in the mirror and what you are looking at around you. What you see is only a small part of who you are. This physical body, though it seems in charge of your existence, is no more than a tool you use to accomplish the tasks needed to complete the mission for which you were born to fulfill, I said with authority and conviction.

I looked around the room to see the student's reactions to what I was saying. All I saw were question marks drawn on their faces. Then a young lady broke the silence and said: *"Are you going to start talking to us about religious nonsense and preach like priests and Sunday TV evangelists? I am fed up with what I hear in church and all the hypocrisy. I hope I did not take this class to hear another sermon"*.

I chuckled at her question. I could not hold in a gentle laugh. My goodness wasn't it but few years back when I used to fire these questions at my guide and teacher, Steven, and see his face light with pleasure. And now this young lady is firing the same questions at me. I hope someday she will allow me to whisper in her ear from my spiritual realm as Steven is whispering in my ears now.

No, my dear I said, I am not going to preach to you, or brainwash you into repeating words that are not yours in order to reach God. There is nothing that I will say that you do not already know at one layer of your awareness or another. I am merely going to assist you in recalling all your knowledge, and help you drop the veil of self-ignorance that you cover your insight with. You are a great shinning gem covered with earthly debris. All I will do is to rub off the accumulation of dirt you gathered through this life and many other lives you lived, so that your brilliant luster will shine through eternity. I cannot make of you what you are not; all I could do is help you create what you choose yourself to be.

"If you are not what you see in the mirror, then what are you? I do not understand. This is my hand, a student said, I see my friends, and I see you. Are you saying I am not a human being? Are you telling me humans do not exist?"

I smiled at my student's impatience that reminded me of myself as a young man eager to absorb all knowledge in a minute's span of time. I looked at my student and said: "I did not say you are not a human being, I said you are not what you see in the mirror; and there is a vast difference between a human being and the physical body you see when you look in a mirror. Take a deep breath my dear and exhale. Close your eyes and tell me what you see?" my student pretended to play the game I asked her to do and said: *"I see nothing"*. I said: "does the light in the room seize to exist just because you do not see it?" My student answered with authority: *"But at this moment it does not exist for me regardless of what is happening in the room and regardless of how many of my friends can see it, the light does not exist for me."* Precisely I said, now open your eyes, do you see the light?

Yes, my student said, *"I can see the light and I can see my body, so why are you telling me that my body does not exist?"*

I did not say that your body does not exist; I replied with a smile, what I said is that you are not what you see in the mirror, you are much more than what you can see, touch, smell, taste and hear. In the simple exercise you just did, you did not see the light when you closed your eyes even though the lights exists, simply because your eyes were closed to the reality of existence of the light in the room even if the light did not exist for you for a moment in time. All you saw was darkness which became your reality at that moment. Precisely as when you look at yourself in the mirror and the only thing you see is your physical body without being aware that a whole universe of energy, power and force exist all around you. You cannot see your thoughts when you look in the mirror, but your thoughts still exist if you see them or not. You cannot touch your imagination, but your imagination is a vital part of your existence. You cannot smell your worries, but not a single day passes without you being worried on one level or another. You cannot hear your happiness, but your happiness exists. You cannot bite, chew or taste your guilt, but your guilt exists. Though you can look into the mirror and see your physical body, you cannot see your emotions, your logic, your intelligence, your mind, your DNA, your genes, your belief system, your passion, your anger, your religious beliefs, your intuition, your inspirations, and most of all you cannot see the energy of life that makes you see your physical body in the mirror.

I looked at my student sitting staring at me in awe of what I said. I could see the wheels of her existence spinning very fast trying to figure out a meaning to all that I said. She cracked a smirk of uncertainty and said: "*I guess there is much more to what I see*". I smiled as I turned back to lessen the impact of my words on her. I remembered myself being stifled as Steven used to lay it heavy on me. I turned back towards my student and said, " relax my Dear, you have two months of class time to figure all this out; but for now, just take a deep breath in and exhale it out in one breath, and with it release the buildup of tension within you. "Let's take a break." I was surprised to see the whole class breathing in and out. I turned back toward my seat and smiled as I heard a sigh of relief coming from around the class.

"So, if you are much more than you see why the same patterns, the same people and the same things keep happening to me? Why do all the other parts of me keep me stuck in the same garbage in my life making me live and do what I do not want to have in my life? Why I am still stuck? Why can't I let go? How can I change?" another student fired at me.

To answer your questions, I replied, it is important to know what a pattern is, and how patterns are formed. It is equally important to know which part of you creates patterns. Then it is very crucial for you to know what it means to get stuck, and why you do get stuck. But before I answer these questions you must take a deep breath, relax and listen to what I am going to say. Make sure to ask me any question if you do not understand what I am saying as you go. Make sure you ask me as many questions as you want until you fully understand what I am revealing to you. I am going to introduce you to a brand-new way of looking at yourself and a new reality about life and living, which will change your perspective about who you are, and will help you realize a new unique perception of yourself.

To start, I will repeat what I said before. You are not what you see in the mirror. What you see with your eyes is only the tool that you use to express your feelings and manifest whatever reality you choose to have in your lives. Your physical body, with a unique name given to you by your parents, regardless of how real it may look, and how intelligent it might sound, and regardless of how sensitive it might feel, it is only an image of all the combined interaction of all the other parts that form the no-name element of your existence. You humans are made of Spirit, a Soul and multiple bodies, each vibrating at a different rate of speed, all connected through spinning energy centers, and all living in a universe of illusion made of time, space and material. I paused for a second and looked around to make sure that all the students are following me; and from the looks on their faces I knew I have lost them.

So, I said: You are all aware of what you touch, see, smell, taste and hear. But what happens to all your physical senses when you daily go into a deep sleep? There is no human alive that did not experience deep sleep at least a thousands of times in a life span; and yet, few truly understand how and why all their physical wants, needs, desires, patterns, addictions, anger, problems, pains, troubles, children, spouses, parents, houses, bank accounts, cars and all their conscious awareness, even the bed on which they are laying, all vanish the instant they fall into deep sleep. Yet though the physical awareness is asleep you survive the unconscious existence. Your heart pumps blood, your liver filters blood, your kidneys filter liquids and you make urine, your intestines extract nutrients from food, and most of all you get rid of billions of dead cells and you create billions of new cells according to a major plan of creation. You will not create a nose cell in your foot neither will you create toe cells on your face. Thus, so far, you have two interrelated physical existences. A conscious existence where you gather information through your physical senses and an unconscious physical existence where you will perform all necessary functions needed to survive as a physical specimen. But the question that you should ask is who is making all these decisions of creation while I am asleep? And what is that power that is forcing the act of creation to be?

I looked around the room and I could hear the silence all around the room.

Then a newly graduated college student said with authority and confidence: *"It is the brain that does all that creation when the physical body is asleep. Every research done by all scientists and doctors confirm that the brain is the source of creation on the physical realm; and the energy which is generated though the chemical reactions of the neurons make all the components of creation to happen."*

I smiled as I watched my student's body language of, *"I got you here"*, and I said, you are correct my dear but to a certain extent. You know that the brain has compartments or storage places of different physical and nonphysical reactions. You also know that the neurons of the brain fire in response to external or internal stimuli. The neurons will react to a physical touch as it reacts to a thought, emotions, logic, intelligence, belief systems, habits, imaginations, will power, anger, frustration, happiness and so on, and stores that response in a specialized compartment. These chemical reactions of the neurons produce electric current that travels through the nervous system and through the endocrine system to cause a certain movement or response in the physical body such as smiling, muscle contractions and expansions, fight or flight, running, dancing and so many other functions you perform daily. But the question to ask is where do these feelings, emotions, logic, imagination, intuition, aspirations, reasoning reside? Where does the brain get its power to function? Where do the chemicals in the brain get its life force so that it can form an electric current from the neurons to activate different components of the body? Can the brain rejuvenate itself, or is it plugged to some power that causes the brain to rejuvenate itself when parts of it are damaged? If the brain has indefinite supply of chemicals to self-generate life, why then does the physical body of a human die? What is death and what is birth and what does the brain have to do with these phenomena? Scientists, researchers and doctors say it is in a portion of the brain called the Mind that is the source of power. This is where pure physical science and awareness split. The brain is a physical component of the physical body, but the mind is a meta-physical energy that impregnates the brain to cause the neurons to fire and commands the physical body to act or react. So, where does the mind reside? What is it composed of? What is its main function?

I took a deep breath and felt the hands of Steven on my shoulders calming me down. I heard his voice in my head saying *"Easy my child, you are not talking to a bunch of scientists. You are addressing fear filled students trying to figure out the basics of how to pursue their happiness in life. They are trying to let go of their problems and are struggling to understand that they have the power to produce different outcomes. Most of all, they are trying to figure out who they are. You already lost them with your explanations. So, go back to your simple explanations of life, your students are waiting for you."*

I truly needed this nudge. It reminded me of the times when Steven used to nudge my forehead with two fingers to remind me to come back to earth when I used to soar with my thoughts so high that made me forget that I barely have feet on this earth. I looked at my students with the compassion of my heart and said: I know I have lost you for a moment, but you are going to be faced with tougher questions from people around you when you try to explain what you are learning in this Awareness class. So be prepared and let me explain again what I have said earlier.

You are not what you seem to see in the mirror. You are composed of many energy vibrations and the thickest of these vibrations is the physical body that you see in the mirror. The other vibrations are also bodies you have, but you cannot see these bodies with our physical senses of seeing, hearing, touching, tasting and smelling because these senses are only made to detect loyour frequency of vibration equal to the vibration of the physical universe. In order to assess the metaphysical body, you must use metaphysical senses such as ESP, Intuition, Clairvoyance, Clairaudience, Clair cognizance, and Clairsentience. These senses vibrate at a higher vibration than the physical body and can detect our metaphysical body with its components mainly the auric outcome of the soul. The Brain run all the functions of the physical body, and the Mind runs all the functions of the metaphysical bodies. The outcome of the interaction between the vibration of the physical and the metaphysical bodies is the etheric body – the house of the Aura - which is a complete replica of the physical body and its organs but is not visible to the naked eye.

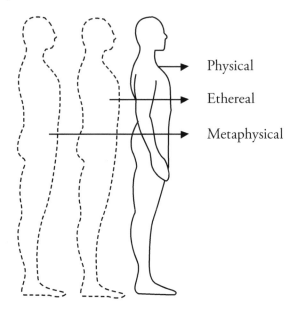

"But why do I feel my emotions in my stomach, my logic in my head and my spirituality in my heart, so where are all these bodies, it sounds too spooky?" A student asked with a look of skepticism all over her face.

Yes you will sense every emotion, logic, thought, aspiration, will power, divine existence which form your whole belief system as physical experiences affecting the physical body. It becomes vital for you to understand what you feel on the physical body is not generated on the physical body. All these feelings are generated in other bodies a human has, (which you will refer to as human metaphysical layers) and translated through the ethereal layer into the physical layer or body. All these human bodies relate to lines of energy called Energy Centers aka Chakras and form what is known as the human body.

In other words, you will consciously become the several realities that your mind constantly generates as it interacts individually and collectively with your emotional, logical and spiritual layers and sub-layers. So whatever feelings you may create as you engage life is the product of what you believe, think, express and perform, which in turn will become the belief system that will automatically guide your daily living forming your patterns, addictions and behavior.

"So, where do all these behaviors reside, and why do I get stuck in my behaviors and patterns, especially when my husband and his family keep pushing my buttons. I know that these behaviors are driving me to absolute anger frustration and anxiety, How can I change and create new feelings when they keep doing the same thing?" Another student asked, *"Why can't I instantly change my behavior when I am faced with all this stupidity?"*

I smiled at her with compassion and said: "How can you change anything in your life when you think that someone else, other than you, is the source of your demise? How can you change what does not belong to you? The moment you give your power-key to someone else to command, they will wield it the way that fits their lives, and your only course of action is to react to them as they yank your reins. To change my dear, you must reclaim your power-key and regain your power again.

"But how can I regain something that I never had in the beginning? Since my early childhood I was told that my whole life has been designed for me and I have no say in whatever happens to me. I only have to be at my best behavior, accept life as it is brought to me, and do my best to deal with it ".

This is precisely why you were born. Your job is to face the tasks of life to fulfill the mission for which you were born; but rather than coping with life, you must start creating your life the way you choose it to be.

"But how can I create my life, or even dare to think that I have a choice in the matter? When I am still living the life of an upper-class slave expected to satisfy everyone's wants, needs and desires; and in return I am offered the prestigious title of a wife, mother or a caretaker. How can I build my own life

when I am expected by parents, society and religion to make everyone else's life a better life?"

I smiled at my student and felt compassion running through the core of my heart. I could see in her eyes the agony of her self-made reality battling with the truth she is trying to attain. A different truth and a new hope might set her free.

Just take a deep breath my dear I said. *(My calm voice came from the depth of the years hearing my teacher calming me down as I got agitated and fired a million questions at him).* Please calm down a bit and listen to me. I know you are feeling lost, confused and agitated. But I promise you that soon all your internal turmoil will start to fade away as you begin to understand who you truly are, why you are on this earth; why you occupied your mother's womb not any other mother's womb. Why you were born to your family, to your religion, to your geopolitical society that governs your emotions, your logic and your spiritual beliefs. You will soon start to understand where you were before you were born, why you were born, and where you will be going after you finish this birth cycle and die. This knowledge will set you free from the bondage of your own self-made feelings that choke life out of you.

But for the time being and moving along, it is very important for you to understand that you are not what you see in the mirror, you are much more than what you see, and all these unseen parts of you determine how you create your qualities and traits, patterns and behaviors, responses and reactions. In totality, it will determine who you are at every moment of your conscious life. This ever-changing YOU is, what is commonly known as, your belief system or your ego. Your ego or your custom designed belief system is what governs your automatic responses in life; it governs your actions and your reactions to any experience you might face, or might create in your daydreaming, as you go in life. It determines the way you live your life and the feelings you automatically generate towards any situation you face. So, in order to change the way you feel in life, you must change your automatic response belief system and reprogram all the data that originally formed your beliefs.

"I truly want to change, that is why I am here listening to you my student fired at me. But how can I change my feelings, when it is the same man, the same parents and the same people in my life; it is the same obligations, the same expectations and the same experiences day in and day out. You say I have the power to reprogram myself, but that is a huge task. I am a total computer illiterate she said as she turned around looking at other students and cracking a smile. How can I change when the experience is still the same and its effects are still the same?"

The illiteracy is not the ignorance of how to program a computer; the ignorance is to believe that your physical existence is all alone in facing your self-made miserable life. The ignorance is to believe that you are powerless to change. The ignorance is to become self-hypnotized by your own self-produced feelings to become paralyzed by your own thoughts, patterns, addictions and reactions to any experience. And the utmost ignorance is to try to change the experience itself rather than changing the way you feel within any experience. You cannot change what others control, but you have the power to change what you control which is the way you generate your feelings towards any experience you face. You do not have to be a computer engineer to reprogram your feelings. A computer engineer is trained to find solutions, and you must start training yourself to produce different solution and start believing that you have the capacity to reprogram your mind to produce different results in any situation you face. All it takes is determination on your part to refuse the feelings you are currently generating towards any experience and determine the new feeling you choose to replace it with. Then focus your mind on bringing new solutions from the super intelligence part of your existence, (your divine soul) rather than depending on automatic responses from the intermingled data of your subconscious which is trying to keep you safe in your misery; thus you will create a new self-controlled calibrated flow of emotional and logical facts that will start reprogramming your subconscious with new data. This powerful process will then allow you to perceive the experiences you constantly face in a completely different way based on how you choose to feel when you face the same experiences in your life day in and day out. Then and only then you will create a new feeling of awareness, expression and empowerment to change the way you act, feel and behave while living with the same husband, parents and people in your life.

I fired my words with such enthusiasm and determination to get my thoughts across. I felt time standing still as the sacred wisdom of life moved through me.

I looked around the class as if I just woke out of a trance, and saw their faces staring at me with glazed eyes as if they are watching a ghost or a UFO. It was a complete silence, not a breath was heard, as if my words were a magical spell sent from the enchanted realm of magic. I looked at Suzanne's face (my assistant) and saw her shaking her head as she always does when I jump in my thoughts and expressions way above what the current class requires. I realized in an instance that I went way above what my students can comprehend at this time of their spiritual understanding and growth. So, I settled myself in my chair and I felt the hand of God running over my forehead, and a tender voice in my ear saying: "Easy my little wandering star this is not the time for this reality, go back to the basics". I regained my senses, and I flashed my usual smile and said jokingly with a tender voice of love and compassion: Wake up guys, this was only a trial run to what you will be discussing in the coming future, but for now let us go back to earth and discuss the basics.

CHAPTER EIGHT

WHO AM I?

I looked at my class with a relaxed inquisitive sense of humor, compassion and love. I just felt the hand of God on my forehead and the voice of my spiritual guide in my mind asking me to start from the basics. I felt a sense of peace travelling through my spine and the hands of God encircling me. Then, and without preparation, a wild thought from the depth of my subconscious came crawling into my conscious mind, and the black wolf started to play its game in me. "You have been teaching the basics to your class all along, so what is Steven talking about now, whispering in my head asking me to restart with the basics"? For a moment, as time stood still, I started to question myself and started feeling humiliated, when suddenly I felt the gentle two-finger nudge on my forehead *(that was the nudge with which Steven used to touch my forehead when as a young man I used to get upset, confused and pissed off at myself as Steven was guiding me, simply because I did not understand what he was saying)* and I heard Steven's familiar sentence ringing in my ears saying *(You idiot why are you doing this to yourself)*. I quickly came back to my senses, and I smiled internally with love as I always do when I feel Steven next to me. I realized that Steven was right. I was running my class as a counseling session and approaching it as an open seminar. I took a deep breath. I relaxed my demeanor and assumed the humbleness of my spiritual teacher Steven when he used to teach me as child and a young man, and now he leads my thoughts as an old man trying to teach the world the ABC's of life, and the power of the mind as it leads us human beings to fulfill the mission for which you are created. I looked around the class and felt the student's eyes fixed on me waiting to hear what I was going to say. I flashed my smile and with soft spoken words I said: When you look in a mirror what do you see? Please engage me and let us all participate. The first answer came from a young lady that usually does not speak and she said smiling: *"I see my gorgeous body and my beautiful face"*. Another said: *"I hate looking at the mirror. I hate all the fat around my body. The mirror is my enemy and so is the weighing scale"*. Another said: *"I look at the mirror to see how old I became"*. Another said: *"I look at the mirror as a daily habit to fix myself"*.

I smiled and said: But whom and what are you seeing in the mirror? And the answer came very swift: *"I see myself"*, *"I see me"*, *"and I see the different parts of my body"*.

And there I flashed my smile because I knew I have the class on the right track of thinking and said: Who is myself and me that you see in the mirror, and can you see all the parts that make up your body? Are there any parts of myself or me that I do not see in the mirror? An answer came flying from the corner of the class with a chuckle: *"I do not see my internal organs"*. Of course, you cannot see your internal organs until someone opens your skin and spill your guts out, I replied with a chuckle; but does that mean that they do not exist if you cannot see them in the mirror? A silence fell over the class and I took this opportunity to ask: Can you see your thoughts in a mirror? Can you see your happiness? Can you see your anger? Can you see your doubt? Can you see your love, hate, emotions, logic, passion, will power? Can you see your weakness, wants, desires, fate, belief, freedom and many more other traits? Of course, you cannot see your other self in a mirror, but your other self is as vital to your existence as a human as your internal organs are vital for your physical body, and without which you cannot be a human. Thus, you as human beings have a physical body that exists in a physical world that you can see in a mirror, and a nonphysical or metaphysical body that resides in a non-physical world that you cannot see in a mirror by the eyes, but you can sense through our insight and feelings. Thus, you can say that you live in two worlds: A physical world and a parallel nonphysical world.

I looked around the class to make sure that the students are following what I was saying, and I saw them all focusing on me trying to soak every word I say. I proceeded to say: As our physical body is composed of many parts, we call organs, that work together under the command of the brain to consciously and subconsciously perform a certain physical task, so is our metaphysical body composed of many parts, we call layers or components, that work together in a very sensitive and intricate manner under the command of the mind to produce certain feelings.

Now, these two parts of a human being, though living in separate worlds communicate consciously, in the awake state, through energy centers, called in the Sanskrit language Chakras or spinning wheels of prayers that spin in a cyclone shape starting its spiral on the metaphysical world, and extending its vortex to touch the physical body in 7 major locations along the physical spine of the physical body, and in 21 minor locations along the face, chest, hands and legs, and in 400 mini locations across the entire physical body called the meridian line. Through the interaction of the different layers of the mind with these energy centers, we form our belief system which governs our conscious existence, thus forming our personalities and controls the vibration of our human souls. The force of life connects the nonphysical world to the physical world through an ethereal cord or tunnel called "The Silver Cord". Through the silver cord life force travels from the divine soul to the human soul. It is always attached to the physical body if the physical body is alive and is only cut at the time of death. During sleep, when the metaphysical body leaves the physical body, it stays connected once again to the physical body by the sliver cord which can expand as far as the human dreams can reach; but when it is time to wake up, the silver cord contracts bringing the metaphysical body in contact with the physical body causing a conscious awareness of the physical world where feelings begin to be formed and physical awareness of the duality of existence start to become real; so that when you look in the mirrors you will know that you are alive.

"But that just doesn't help me much. What you are saying does not help my confusion about God, prayer and religion. I am really confused. Would you please tell me how to change? I cannot take it anymore." A student fired at me. I saw her red face and the veins popping out of her forehead, and a tear forming in the corner of her eyes holding itself by pride from trickling down her cheeks.

A flash of my own childhood confusion rushed through my vision, when I fired many questions at my teacher Steven and all I got from him was a gentle warm smile that always calmed me instantly. I flashed my smile and looked at my student with compassion, love and understanding; and with calmness of the ages that encircles me I said: Take a deep breath my dear friend and calm down. Remember you are in this awareness class to learn how to fish and find your answers, rather than depending on me to give you a fish and offer you the answer. The first rule in discovering your own power, to create your own answers to all your questions, is to understand the energy mechanics that form your feelings of confusion and certainty. So, listen to me a little longer and try to understand all I am saying, because it is going to be the basis on which you can build your answers to most of your questions.

So, as I said before, you live in two adjacent worlds connected through life forming energy centers. You live in a permanent metaphysical world which is the house of our soul, our mind and our emotions, and a temporary physical world which is the house of our brain and our physical body.

Between these two worlds exists a life force energy that sends life to the physical body through the chakras to enable the physical existence to create certain feelings as it faces predetermined experiences and while performing certain tasks and transfers back to the metaphysical world the results of these feelings. Whatever feelings you create as you face life on this earth determines the outcome of where your human soul will be. You either vibrate at the vibration of the Divine Soul to merge with the Divine Spirit, or you will remain earth bound suffering with the illusion of our temporary physical existence.

"But what does that mean? Are you saying that I am responsible for creating the feelings I produce? Every feeling I have is determined by people, circumstances and situations. If they treat me well, I feel good, and if I am treated bad, I feel bad. So why are you saying it is I who determines how I feel? It is this stinking life that is causing my stress, anxiety, and sadness? Blaming us is not fair? A student fired at me.

Yes, my dear, it is you, and you alone that determine how you feel and how you respond to activities, experiences and stimuli you face in your life. You are the master of your own outcomes. You are the creator of your feelings by the way you choose to live and act and respond to your emotions as you face situations in your daily living. Remember you chose to come to this earth from the realm of the spirit, formed a physical body in your mother's womb, then came out to this temporary physical air breathing earth only to refine the past feelings you carried with you from a previous life, still residing in your soul or subconscious data bank. Your job is to produce new grand feelings and replace the past life old feelings before you move on.

In simpler terms, you chose to come back again to this physical material world as a Human Soul, simply because it gives you the best physical training you can have to refine your emotions and produce the best feelings you can muster always measuring your outcome with the grand yard stick

71

of feelings the Divine Soul. Your Human Soul is the data bank of all the feelings you produce through the many lives you lived before. Your goal is to reach the vibration of the Divine Soul that are necessary for you to move on to higher stages of existence.

I looked around at the students, and it felt as if they were in a daze. Not a single word or expression came out. I looked at Suzanne as she shrugged her shoulders. I felt as if I revealed the secret of life, and no one could understand it. Then a sweet voice broke the ice as she said:

Then all that we are doing on this earth is developing a feeling towards anything we face and experience in life. Are you saying that it is the feelings we produce towards anything we face in this life, regardless of what it is, and regardless how tough or easy it is will determine our next stage of existence after we die?

Yes, it is my dear, and throughout history great teachers came to this earth to teach us how to accomplish that and produce heaven on earth. But you ignore these simple rules and you remain stuck in your survival mode. You ignore basic principles of life and living; simple principles such as love, gratitude, forgiveness, belief and faith. You get stuck in your multi religions, repeating words of prayers hoping that these words can lead you to Heaven without understanding what heaven is, or what is hell, or what and who is God; clinging on to physical living, afraid to die or go home. You live in a complete state of amnesia to the basic facts that you are on this earth to prepare the necessary feelings needed for your next life in the spirit world as divine souls.

So, who is God, and who is god's God another student fired from the corner of the class?

God is the energy of creation. God is not a man or a woman. God is the energy of life. You cannot think of God from a physical or human perspective or else you will never understand. God is the energy of all life forces; the easiest way to understand is to think of a battery, it is not the metal that contains the battery that makes it work, it is the power of the electric current with the battery that produce the necessary force to make the battery work. God is not a finite force. God is the energy of life that permeates the multiverse creations into existence. So, when you speak about God you do not speak about a physical entity that possess human traits. In your wildest speculation you can only imagine what this power and it its force might be.

So, when you as humans pray to God, you are not praying to a man living on cloud number # 9, with a book of good and evil in his hand, either he sends you to a physical place called heaven or roasts you in a place called hell. You pray hopping that God will have mercy upon you when you die. You repeat words and sentences that you do not understand just to please God. You go by the manmade understanding of God, rather than truly living by the knowledge that you are one with God living this earthly realm to affirm your divinity. You live as if you are the slaves of a man called God hoping that God will have mercy upon you. The grandest mistake you will ever make, as you live this earthly realm, is to think that you are separate from the Grand creating energy, and that you are here on this earth just to please a man called God.

All you have to know and understand at this stage of existence is that your job as a human is to form the grandest feelings you can produce, using the power of creation that you have from the grand power of creation that you call God to be able to reach the next stage of existence, where grand feelings are the norm of being, not the physical life.

Now this being said, you are not alone in this fake physical mess. There also exist alongside of you Great Spirit assistants, motivators, and great cheerleaders rooting for you, and helping you to achieve your tasks on this earth, regardless of the physical, emotional and mental obstacles you face. You call these energies Angels that are from the spirit realm but never incarnated. And at the same token there are the spiritual motivators that provide you with physical emotional mental and spiritual situations, experiences, and problems, for you to overcome the problems and find the grandest feelings you can generate while living within these tough situations. You call these trying energies Demons.

When earthly living becomes tough to endure, other higher spiritual help comes from the Archangels. Archangels such as Michael, Raphael, Gabriel and many others. These Archangels do not interfere in your daily living until you ask for their help. At the same token when you allow your thoughts of earthly physical accomplishments to be at the forefront of your mind, and you think that you got great results with the loving Archangels, you will be exposed to great temptations by another powerful Archangel, the devil. So, if you are alive on this physical earth you are always physically, emotionally and mentally tempted to stay earthbound and forget about why you really did incarnate or were reborn to this earth again. It is always your choice in this earthly living; whatever side of the living balance you choose to be in, will always determine the feelings you manifest and be in the grandest task you will always face in every moment of our existence.

So why do we really pray, and how do we pray? Why did Jesus teach the Lord's Prayer? The same student asked with a grin.

If you really study the Lord's Prayer in Aramaic which is the original language Jesus spoke you will see it is the greatest tool by which you can accomplish the tasks for which you were born to this earth, and that is again to be in the grandest feelings you can ever be. This grand communication starts by acknowledging that you are one with God and that you are from the same spirit. You understand your tasks on Earth the fake reality, and you will always bring the grandest feelings of Heaven (the divine soul of feelings) to our daily earthly living.

Now I am really confused! fired a student sitting in front of me who has not said much since the beginning of the class. If I am supposed to be a representation of God on this earth, why am I unable to heal the pain in my spine which many doctors say I might need surgery to fix. Though I pray every night I ask God why must I endure this pain, what have I have done to deserve this? Could you please explain why God does not listen to me, and help me heal without a surgery?

I smiled as I looked deeper into her eyes, and the voice of my teacher Steven echoed in my head, it is about time Suhail to say it, but be gentle, for they might not understand. I looked around at my students in class waiting for my answer. I wondered if it was really time to teach the great powers innate in every human, lying dormant, waiting for every human to wake up to his and or hers destiny to be the God of the universe you call man and woman; and to create the living they choose to live in. I wondered if the class will understand what I will say, as I felt the soothing hand of Maryam my angel rubbing the back of what is left of my hair, and the voice of my teacher pushing me to proceed.

I took a deep breath as if I am entrusting a long-kept secret. I said: Before you indulge and go deeper into the Enhanced Healing Powers, let us understand some basic terms that many are confused about and they interpret according to their own needs and pleasure. But Before I could start, I was taken back to the class reality by a student firing at me.

Before you move ahead, I have several serious questions that are really bothering me and couple of my friends with me here in class. Why do I get mad, get sad, and many times I get happy or get excited about different things? Am I insane? Many times, you asked us to release. To take a deep breath and release. So, what is release? What does it mean to release? How do I release? How do I change, how do I let go? How can I deal with those emotions and feelings and those already built-in stories within me that make me do what I don't want to do? Or simply make me do what I do without even knowing why I am doing it.

I smiled and said; It does not matter what you do automatically, though it has a great impact on your life. These automatic responses of mad, sad, happy and excited are built into your subconscious. These data or feelings become an engraved data into your automatic hard drives and core values, which in turn become your daily response to any experience or situation you might face in living this life. You must recognize this important fact about yourself, and release yourself from your accumulated data and your automatic responses. Your obsolete data installed in you by your parents, schools, social life in this present life and especially also coming in from past life experiences acknowledge what no longer works for you. You must delete it and release it. but this is not enough; you must start to replace it with new data that does work for you depending on the choices you create and the feelings you choose to feel regardless of the story you might face in your daily living, and that is how you can Change. You must learn how to live this life by the power of the Super Mind, the problem solver the powerful creator of feelings and emotions, creating a new reality to every new experience you face. you must create your own emotions; it is not the experience the creates the way you feel. You must learn how to release your automatic reactions, and instantly develop new actions to anything you face, simply to be able to create whatever feeling you choose at any moment you are faced with a new decision.

My Friends, I will interrupt my discussion of the Advanced Power for a little while, and before I answer your many questions, before I go any further in this powerful discussion, I still see a lot of confusion on your faces by the way you are asking your questions. I feel a major part of our discussions still needs more explanation and a better clarification. So now, let us take some time to relax and focus. I want you all to interact with me and participate in this upcoming discussion. I am going to ask you all a simple question and I want you all to freely express your ideas about this subject. Then when you are ready, I will introduce to you a very beautiful, powerful technique, a technique to release. Simply it is The Art of Release.

My questions to you through all these meetings and classes will always be: Who are you? Who do you truly think you are? And I hope you can honestly tell me whatever you think you are.

One by one all in the room started to freely express who they are, and the summation of their answers of who they are centered about their genders, their relationships, their husbands, wives, children, work, status, income, diseases, sorrows, pains, frustrations, anxieties, worries, concerns, achievements, academic successes, goals, plans, desires, obligations, duties but no one said who they think they truly are. I smiled and said: I did not ask you about your relationships, your aspirations, your status, your ailments, your fears, your problems, your solutions, successes and your dreams. I simply asked who are you? And to make it a bit interesting my accompanying question is: Why are you on this earth and what are you doing here?

You can tell me stories from history about how humans evolved from being homo-erectus to homo-sapiens through thousands of years. Generation after generation going through the advancement of living, through wars and disasters, through great times and advancements of traveling and communications. But you did not tell me who you truly are. What are you doing here on this earth?

Why were you born? Is there a certain reason for your birth or is it something that happened haphazardly, when a male sperm impregnated a female egg? Do you all have some things to do on this earth? Is it the same for all humans, or each human has a different task to achieve? Who are you, and why are you here?

My friends, you must truly start to understand the basis of who you truly are and what are you doing here on earth. Before you just start living without a direction, wondering without any aim, just dealing with living as it happens, wandering about what else to do, and before you can just move from one realm to another realm you must understand who you are and what you are doing on this earth.

Thousands of religious books have been written about this subject, and hundreds upon hundreds of religions sprang up through times immemorial each with hundreds of denominations each claiming to be the truth. But if the truth is one, why all these religions? The simple answer is that their truth is their own judgement of the true reality.

So, it is no wonder that each one of you gave me a different answer of who you are. You based your answers on your own judgements of what is important to you, and on the truths that you were taught, and brainwashed to belief that it is yours, when it is truly someone's else's truth of who you are and what are supposed to act and be.

You accepted a fake truth of some authority over you rather than searching inside your inner realms to find your own truth. To live this earth with the grandest feelings of happiness, love and peace, you must erase the dust which has camouflaged your own universal truth by years and ages of fake judgements and falsehoods. You must discover your internal shining light that will brighten your reality for many lives realms and stages to come, on this earth and beyond.

Do not feel bad my friends, I am not here to depress you. I am talking to you to tell you that you have the power within you to know the ultimate non-judgmental truth of who you truly are. All you must do is start pealing all the layers of fake judgmental truths that you accumulated from books, religions, parents and situations you faced in this live and in many passed lives. You formed many fake emotions and feelings in response to various experiences and situations you were faced with, but you always have the power to change your mind and choose a different way to feel.

So, who are you, and what are you doing on this earth? The answer is simple. You are a Being living this earth for the fun of experiencing. To form the grandest feelings regardless of the experience or situation you face. You are on this earth simply for the joy of the experience.

To enjoy the Experience, you must learn the Art of releasing your own obstacles that hinder your success.

CHAPTER NINE

THE ART OF RELEASE

Before you start discussing this powerful subject of release, let me define what is release and why it is an art.

Release in simple terms mean to liberate to let loose to let go.

Self-release to set the self-free.

The art of: Basically means, the skill and the technique of creating and expressing in a refined majestic form of the mind and the heart.

So, what is this art of release? What is this very beautiful, powerful technique to release. How do you release, how do you change, how do you let go? Why you must release, and what are you releasing? How can you deal with those emotions and feelings and those already built-in stories within you that can make you automatically, without thinking do whatever you do not want to do, or do what you do automatically without even knowing why. Your lives are so automatic, and all you do is to instantly react to everything you face without hesitation. You get mad, you get sad, and maybe you get happy or excited about whatever you are faced with. It is so automatic you do not question it until it no longer makes you feel good about yourself. Then you wonder why you cannot create the living you want to live, and why your life is a mundane routine.

My friends, it does not matter what you do automatically without thinking when faced with any provocation in your living. What really matters is you must master the art to release your automatic reactions or actions to your embedded stories and learned data, and be able to create whatever feelings and emotions you choose, at any moment you choose, regardless of what you are faced with, or the situation you are confronting.

Thank you for bringing out this subject. A student said to me. I have been struggling with my emotions since my young teenager daughter died couple years ago. I cannot seem to get over it. Please teach me how to release this pressure and sadness within me and learn how to communicate with her without pain. I know she wants to talk to me, but I cannot seem to overcome my pain of losing her.

I looked at her with compassion and said; take a deep breath my dear and listen to the rest of this class, and if you still have more questions, come see me in my office after the class, and you can talk deeper and more private if you choose.

But for now, my friends, please understand that all humans living this earth are faced with experiences in which they all define their core feeling and values of what is good, what is bad, what's wrong and what is right. Values about what they should do and how they should feel and what to accept or reject as they move on their journey of personal daily living. These feeling might coincide with others or not, it really does not matter.

What matters to you is that these learned values are the basis of your personal daily actions and or reactions to experiences you are faced with. They are the result of your upbringing, your parent's teachings and your schooling. In general, your core values and the way you produce your emotions and your feelings depend upon the society you born into and the society you live in now. And more, it depends about who taught you what, and the lessons you taught yourself in response to the severity of the reaction you created when faced with all experiences you faced from your mother's womb to the daily affairs of the life you are currently living. Regardless which part of the world you lived or live in, and your socio-economic situation you were born to, or currently you live in.

That is why you constantly say, when facing any experience or situation in your daily living "this is me", "this is who I am". But truly what you are saying is; this is the way I react to the values that had been installed in me, and embedded in my subconscious by my own reaction to past experiences, and by the way I was programed by parents, schools, society, religion and my economic situation and upbringing. Truly you are not creating your own emotions and feeling, you are just repeating what you have been programed to feel towards any situation. But my friends, you are totally forgetting why you were born to this earth. Always remember as you move through your daily living, you are on this earth to face new or repeated experiences to create the grandest emotions and feelings regardless how tough or simple the experience might be.

But, as you face the experiences of living, you rely solely on the accumulated data from past experiences. You become emotional. You activate your emotions based on previous results to experiences, regardless if it is good or bad. You generate your fight or flight mechanisms to protect yourself from physical, emotional, mental and spiritual harm. You produce old judgements residing in your subconscious data bank accumulated by all the learned constant input by parents, schools, friends and society, or from the way you judged yourself as you faced situations as a child or the adult that you are. But truly all you are doing is repeating what other people of authority in your life taught you to do, rather than creating a new calm emotional feeling of your own in response to what you are facing. Now release yourself from your old prejudged data and liberate yourself from old feelings. Just simply refuse to allow the old preprogramed you to run the new you. Refuse to allow the child and the old weak part of you to run the woman or the man that is currently you. Stop sabotaging yourself rather than allowing yourself to live in the agony of fear of what might happen or will happen. Give yourself permission to try something different.

The severity and quality of your emotions when facing an experience totally depend on your judgement of what you are currently facing. Your emotional outcome is directly linked to the severity of the story stored in your data banks about a similar situation. The stories that you carry about people that have passed in your life alive or dead, incidents and accidents, experiences and situations generate instant emotions and feelings of love and hate, fear and courage, disgust or happiness, are no more than obsolete stories that you must release. You will always remember the story, but its effect on your current daily living will fade away, as you create a new judgment of the experience you now are facing, and your feelings will change to whatever level you choose to be in.

The feelings that you create on this earth will determine your status as a human being. So do not run away from your feelings. Do not bury them within your old obsolete files. Do not be afraid to tackle them. When your feelings flair up, take a moment to address them. Take a deep breath and calm yourself down. Use different terminology when you talk to yourself. Think of the now, and how do you choose to feel in the moment. You have so much power and so much creative energy to be able to create the feeling you choose to have regardless of the story within you, and regardless of the experience you are facing. You are the lord of your creations, it is not the situation or the experience that determines how you feel, it is your mind that creates the power of your feelings.

What you are saying is great and I understand that I have the power to release. But could you please tell me how do I release? What method should I use? I have tried to meditate but I failed. I tried Yoga, but it did nothing for me to change my feelings. I read many books, I imagined myself in a different feeling, but it did not work. I used affirmations and it felt like I was repeating useless words. I am still sad, I am still afraid, and I still hate to wake up in the morning afraid of what I am going to face this day. I took this class hoping I would learn a practical approach, not just theory. Please help me. You are my only alternative I can run to. Please give me a step by step how this is done. A lady sitting a pace away from me said.

My dear friend, I know that you are struggling with the stories within you. You are allowing the stories of the past to dictate all the feelings and emotions you are automatically creating. You are saying that you want to change but you cannot. You are running after tools of meditation and affirmations to help you change, but before you can find the tool, you must determine the goal. And in your case, the goal is to look at all the obsolete data in your automatic hard drive, or your subconscious mind and decide to get rid of all fear, anger, anxiety, personal hurt, and bad traumas in your life since childhood, or even from past lives. The moment you determine to get rid of the past feelings, and make it the goal of your life, then you will find the suitable tool to use to help you release. But this is not enough. It is this last part that will do the trick. It is dedication and constant work to achieve your goal.

You must dictate to yourself how you choose to feel when faced with any situation. You cannot ignore what automatically comes out of you. You cannot dismiss these feelings. You cannot run away from your automatic feelings. The moment you run away from your destructive feelings, they will follow you all your life causing major anxiety and depression. But the moment you face your embedded feelings, the moment you decide to introduce a new powerful light of logic, wisdom and love to whatever you are facing the automatic feelings will start to fade away. You will introduce new genuine feelings of your choice. You will decide how you choose to feel at every moment, and your new feelings will dominate your demeaner regardless of how tough or simple the situation you are facing.

But this is a very difficult thing to do. I have been trying to control my emotions and feelings, but it is very difficult. It takes me hours to calm down, and sometime many days, especially when it affects my family, my job and my relationships in general. I have tried to follow many self-help articles, but I am still upset afraid of what next is going to happen to me. Another student fired at me.

I turned towards her and said: You are using tools without the understanding of what is going on in your life. You are trying anything hoping that one of them will work. Though you want to get rid of your problems and the bad feelings that constantly haunt you, you are only playing the game of hit or miss hoping that one of the tools you use will relieve your symptom of constant fear and anxiety. You never took the time to deeply analyze your automatic data that is playing havoc with your emotions as you move through your life span. You are trying many tools because someone told you to so, hoping that eventually you would find one that may help you temporarily to relax.

My dearest friend, you will only relieve your pains, fears and anxiety when you decide to face all the dormant beliefs that cause your emotional turmoil and delusional feelings.

Truly I say to you, until you choose to review the self-made fake stories that you live by, until you decide to release the limiting beliefs that you accumulated through the years, you will never set yourself free. It is your diligent work to master your own feelings which will eventually set you free. Simply blindly utilizing someone's prescribed general tool, regardless of what the tool might be, to cure your symptoms of anxiety and fear will not set you free. These tools will only give you suggested temporary relief. But when you truly choose to release your bottled feelings you must choose to do the work.

- When you choose to permanently change your limited perceptions of who you are and determine to deeply investigate your emotions and feelings.
- When you open your own inner sense of self-worth and understand that your mind is an extension of the Universal Power of Creation, you will then determine the reality of every judgement you perceived as real within your life span and make the appropriate changes.
- When you believe in the power of your capability to change.
- When you recognize that your problems are your own doings no one else.
- When you acknowledge that your emotional outcomes are your own creations.
- When you have faith that what you choose is already done.
- When you realize that you are the only one that has the power to create new feelings.
- When you apply the power of your wisdom of logic and compassion, all wrapped up in your great vibration of self-love then and only then you change the emotional outcome of every story you have accumulated through the years.

This is my friend the basis of the power to heal, the basis of the Art of Release, the essence of your Self-Creation formula.

Thank you for this explanation, but could you please give me some more specific steps that I can use to daily to help control to my messed up emotions. I am not asking for tools, but for baby steps to help me on my way… my student said with a grin on her face…

I laughed as everyone in the room laughed at her subtle remark and said: Of course, my dear, I will give you steps to follow. But regardless of what I say, until you feel the grand feeling of change within you to overcome your old self and discover the power of creation within you, all the steps I will give you will become another tool of hit or miss that you will use as you have used many tools in the past but to no avail.

So here it is, please take notes and we will discuss the steps as you go. These steps are very important to follow to get rid of the limiting stories you constantly tell yourselves, and the limiting beliefs that you form out of feelings you generated as reactions to stories you faced or heard of at one time or another.

You store all the events, emotions, feelings and judgments you generated at a certain time in the past, in deep files in your subconscious mind. These files are always ready to surface as an outdated story, simply to protect you from the same expected danger, pain, shame or trauma you felt before, when you consciously face any new similar situation. The subconscious does not recognize time. Feelings that occurred in childhood, or even in past lives due to a previous story, are readily accessible to your conscious mind at any moment you are faced with a similar story.

The more the stories of the events are recalled, you generate an upgraded mixed story that differs by time only from the original event that happened in the past, adding new imagined details and causing your emotions and feelings to grow without restrictions, thus causing your story to become more profound and your feelings to sore with no control causing you fear, anxiety, depression and sickness.

Now with your new determination to free yourself and using the Art of Release, you must get rid of these stories. They belong to the past to a different version of who you are today.

When you really get rid of the story about what happened in the past, then your emotions and your feelings will change; allowing you to live by how you choose to feel today, not by how the innocent incapable child within you is still dictating to you how to live, feel and act.

The key to get rid of the Story is to use these combined powerful techniques developed from time immemorial:

1. Identify the damage that the story is causing in your current life. Write it down see it and think of it.
2. Decide that the old story has no effect on you today and it must be changed. Engage the grand creative power of your mind and understand that you have created this story and you have the power to get rid of it.
3. Visit the true origin of the story. Travel with your memory through time to the origin of the story.
4. Do not be afraid. Do not allow your fear to prevent you from visiting the origin of the story when it truly happened regardless of how embarrassing, fearful or hurtful it might have been. It is a story of the past that happened to a much younger, frightened, weaker and unexperienced part of you.
5. See the story as a third person watching the event on a screen. As if you are watching it on a TV screen or movie theater. Imagine yourself going into the screen to the little you. Stand behind the fearful child that is a younger you. Hug yourself and say: I will never allow anyone to hurt you again. I am with you forever.
6. Step out of the screen with the love of the child in your heart. Bring the image of the past hurt with you. Minimize the image

you see. Make a black and white pale picture of the image with no life to it. Put this lifeless image into a small insignificant frame. Hang the frame on the wall of memories, strip it from any power or meaning. Repeat this process several times until the effect of the past is totally gone.

7. See the event with compassion rather than anger.

8. Mostly forgive yourself for allowing this event to still have power over you.

9. Acknowledge your power as you look at the event you just overcame and hanged on the wall. Repeat to yourself: "By the power of the universal power within me, no traumas of the past or present, or its causes will have any power over me anymore. I once was weak, and I allowed these traumas to take advantage of me. But no more; no traumas and no human from the past or the present will have any power over me and the way I feel till the end of time".

10. Believe within your heart and mind that the story is gone. And Have faith it is gone.

11. Identify the new lesson to be learned.

12. Live and act with power and have faith that you can create whatever feelings you choose.

This is the gateway to the Art of Release. Adopt it as the way for personal success. Change your judgements of any self-accepted reality. Live in peace, and never be afraid to change.

CHAPTER TEN

ENHANCED HEALING POWERS

I guess it is the time to go back and discuss the Healing Powers that I postponed a while ago simply to discuss the Art of Release first to find your own internal reality.

But before you can go further, let me explain some basic terminology.

What is Healing? Healing is the process of the restoration of health or reality on the physical, emotional, mental and spiritual realms from unbalanced, self-inflicting fake realities, diseased, damaged or unvitalized organism or disturbance of the waves of the subatomic quanta. Healing is completely different than curing. **Curing** is eliminating all evidence of a disease; while healing is becoming whole as a unit on the physical, emotional, mental and Spiritual realms. Healing activates all the energies of the waves and particles that compose us as single but connected individual universes known as human beings. The body has an inherent capacity to heal because of its connection to the perfect energy of creation. When you have a cut on our finger, or any part of our physical body, somehow our sub atomic quanta waves of energy works with our quarks that compose the basis of our cells and tissues to create a healing energy that reconstruct our cells to magically heal the cut. When you break a bone, it is not the doctors that ultimately heal the break; it is our innate God like power within our cells that do the healing. You can see the wound and the break heal, but you have no conscious idea of how the healing happened. You know how powerful the healing capacity of the mind can be especially in the placebo effect, and how powerful the healing is when you believe and have faith in a new reality though nothing physically was given to the physical. You all heard of miraculous healings that traditional doctors cannot explain which you call miracles. But how can you consciously and consistently activate and intensify this innate healing potential? That is what you will learn shortly as you engage the Enhanced Healing Powers.

I thought you are going to make it easier to understand, but you are using scientific words that means nothing to us, could you please explain what you just said in terms that we humans could understand. For what you just said, my priest will for sure condemn you to hell.

I smiled as the class burst into laughter and said: No, my dear your priest has no power to condemn me or you or anyone else to hell. You and I and every other living human on this earth, alone and only, have the power to create any reality we choose. We can create hell on earth as we can create heaven on earth. We have the power to be whatever we choose to be, We are the masters of our own destinies and the creators of our fates not your priests, gurus, yogis, or any self-proclaimed power. We have the free will to exercise God's innate power in us and create our solid reality. However, when we are consumed with fear, doubt and anger, we give our power away to some, god, emblem, religion, habit, dogma and or ritual and enslave our realities to fake powers hoping for a better result. But my dearest, no one has more powers than you to heal yourselves and create the life you choose for yourself.

To answer your original concern, I will write down some explanations of some basic scientific components of the human anatomy and give them to you as a reference to understand how the healing power occurs in you.

What is the universe? The universe is defined as all existing matter in space and time as a whole, and all of energy in its various forms, including dark energy which is what holds life together, the essence of life, electromagnetic radiation, matter, waves and particles of the quanta, the subatomic energy of life that exist in the universe.

What is a Cell: The cell is the basic structural and functional unit of any living thing? Each cell is a small container of chemicals and water wrapped in a casing. There are 100 trillion cells in a human, and each contains all of the genetic information necessary to manufacture a human being. Each cell is made up of molecules and our molecules are made up of atoms.

What are Atoms: Atoms are extremely small and are made up of a few even smaller particles. It is estimated that there are 7 trillion atoms in the human body. An atom consists of a central nucleus that is usually surrounded by one or more electrons. Each electron is negatively charged. The nucleus is positively charged and contains one or more relatively heavy particles known as protons and neutrons. The electron orbits around the proton with an unknown energy that scientists call the Dark Energy and Dark Matter. This powerful energy holds the atom together as it holds the universe together. It gives the human atoms a frequency unique to the type of atom it is and gives the vast universe its existence. If you examine our inner space, you discover that it is very much like outer space. You think it is really made up of vast amounts of nothingness, but that's incorrect. For the nothingness is made up of Dark Energy, or Creative Energy both within the inner space of our bodies and the vast distances of outer space. Everything in the universe is made up of atoms, same as the human body. You know that energy and matter make up less than 5 percent of the universe and that the rest of the universe is made up of dark energy and dark matter simply referred to as the creative power of God that holds the universe together. Atoms fit together with other atoms to make up matter.

It takes a lot of atoms to make up anything. Each different kind of atom makes up an element.

What is Subatomic: subatomic particles are the fundamental makeup of an atom. An atom has a nucleus, which is its center, or core. The nucleus contains subatomic particles: protons and neutrons. Protons are positively charged particles. Neutrons are neutral particles. Surrounding the nucleus is a cloud of very small subatomic particles called electrons. Electrons are negatively charged particles.

What is a Particle: A particle is a small object that has several physical or chemical properties such as volume, density or mass? A particle occupies a well-defined position in space e.g. a grain of sand. Every physical matter like atoms and molecules and subatomic particles is made of particles. Particles vary in size and quantity objects depending on their density, such as powder granules to humans moving in a crowd or celestial bodies in motion.

What is a Wave: Waves have no definite position? A wave is spread out in space, it carries with its energy related to the frequency of its motion. On throwing a stone in a pond of water, the waves start moving out in the form of concentric circles. Similarly, the sound of the speaker reaches everybody in the audience.

What is a Quark: A quark is the elementary particle and a fundamental ingredient of matter? Quarks combine to form Protons and Neutrons the basic components of an atom.

What are Quanta: Quanta is the plural for Quantum. It is the Latin word for amount. It is the smallest possible discrete unit of any physical entity involved in interaction or a motion, such as energy or matter. The energy of each quantum is directly proportional to the frequency of the motion.

The quantum energy of a human atom is called the electron of an atom which is in constant motion. In case of light the quantum of energy is called a "photon". A photon is a single quantum of light. Light and other electromagnetic energy is absorbed or emitted in quanta or packets.

What is DNA: DNA is short for deoxyribonucleic acid. It is a long molecule that contains the unique genetic code of organisms that determines all the characteristics of a living thing. *DNA* is the hereditary material in humans and almost all other organisms. Like a recipe book it holds the instructions an organism needs to develop live and reproduce.

What are Genes: A gene is the basic physical and functional unit of heredity. It is a unit of heredity which is transferred from a parent to offspring and is held to determine some characteristic of the offspring. Every person has two copies of each gene, one inherited from each parent. Genes are made up of DNA. Some genes act as instructions to make molecules called proteins.

What is Genetic Code: The *genetic code* is a set of instructions that direct the translation of DNA into 20 amino acids, the basic units of proteins in living cells.

But what does this all mean? Said another student and how can you use this power to heal?

To heal my dear, you must believe and have faith that you are one with God; that the energy within you is the same energy of creation that created this physical universe and the multi trillion universes around. You must understand and have faith that the whole external universe, that you observe some of it stars at night, is the same universe that a subatomic particle inside your body sees when looking at you from the inside. What you see on the outside is the same that is in the inside, and the power that holds the universe together is the same power that holds your whole body together.

Could you please explain it a little bit further, a student said from the back corner of the class? You are the first person that says I and God are one, I do not have to fear God, I do not have to worship God, but I must acknowledge that God and I are one.

But be careful my dear in what you are saying. Unless you use the powerful triangle of creation (Power, Wisdom and Love) your creations will lack the essence of healing and will become a vague physical power that will burn you. I will explain this process a bit later.

What is the Universal God Healing Power?

Universal Healing Power is a universal energy technique combined with Universal Quantum Energy which is the Creative Power of God known by science as the Dark Energy found in every cell, atom, molecule, system and organ in our physical body and in the vast universe and multi universes. This is the most advanced Self-understanding, self-Expressing and Empowering healing modality. It realizes the power of your connection to the universe effectively functioning on the subatomic quanta of existence to form a powerful potent healing modality that brings Heaven to Earth.

In simpler terms, it is not enough to affirm the power of God in healing, it is very important to become this healing power and realize yourself as an intricate part of the healing. You are no more a conduit through which the universal energy flows; you are the source of this powerful healing energy as being an extension of the universe operating and existing as a human by the power of the Dark Energy and matter, which is the Creating Energy of God.

Wow that is a different way of thinking, a student said, can I really do that?

I smiled and said: The moment you realize that you are the healing energy, then you are not praying and hoping that some foreign energy might flow through you, you are becoming the God energy and every part of your existence is energy that flows at precise formulated frequency depending on the status of your emotions, feelings, and the triangle of creation that you are operating from; Power, Wisdom and Love.

Look at yourself. What power are you using to manage your daily living? What wisdom are you applying in your daily living? Is your heart full of unconditional love? Or simply you are operating from physical need, want and desire in the name of love. What are your stories? What are your limitations? What are your automatic responses to life and living? Answers to these basic questions will determine the frequency and potency of your healing flow when trying to supply healing conditions to yourself or to another human, animal or a plant.

This is tough to do when all your life you have been told differently, a student said. What must I do to change?

The beliefs you hold about yourself and the world, your emotions, your memories, and your habits all can influence your mental and physical health. These connections between what is going on in your mind and heart, and what is happening in your body, form the roots of health and disease.

Which reality are you living in? What are your core values and your beliefs? Do you really understand and realize who you are? It is not important to repeat affirmations, prayers and words that someone spoke thousands of years ago; what is important is to realize yourself within every word you speak, to realize the power of your connection to whom or what you are praying to; and to have faith that the power of the energy that you are allowing to flow through the subatomic waves and particles of your own physical body will determine the power of healing energy that you are administering to yourself or to others.

Can I really accomplish that? Will I be able to create the miracle of healing in my life?

Thoughts and emotions carry vibrations that impact your physical state. At a physical level, the body is made up of atoms and water, which are in a constant state of motion. Science has demonstrated that high vibrational thoughts, words, feelings and music can change the crystal structure of water and cells which can change their function. Recognizing that you are the source of positive, kind, and inspiring thoughts and emotions vibrating in harmony with the universe and with your cells since they share a similar frequency, will allow your physical body to function at its optimal state. In fact, when you are one with God's universal creative energy, sending the type of vibrations or energy patterns that are carried by certain words, intentions and love, you are able to cause physical changes in you DNA structure, which in turn will affect how the genetic code to change the building blocks of your body are formed. But by sending damaging words, feelings, intentions and hate you are mainly feeding radical cells which are unstable atoms that can damage the body's cells, causing illness and aging.

You are an extension of the source of creation. You are not a separate entity that is living this earth by chance. You are not a puppet that someone called god plays with, manipulates for his or her own pleasure. You are a true extension of the Power of creation. You are the power of creation vibrating at a lower frequency to be able to experience this earth's duality and still create the best energy of feelings that you can assemble. The fact that you can change your mind about anything while you are living this earth indicates that you have the power to create a new reality every moment of your living. So, you know that you are a creator utilizing the infinite power to create your reality as you choose.

Oh my God, I cannot believe I have been living my life with all my fears to upset God and my family, living with anxiety that god is upset with me, because I am a sinner.

But now my dear, knowing this fact of unity and oneness, you can utilize this powerful fact into bringing enough energy to be able to create solutions and new outcomes as needed; giving every outcome enough energy to create a new realty. Then you must also understand that nothing is done to you, you have the power to create your realities the way you allow yourself to respond to experiences in living. If you allow yourself to diminish your powerful energy of creation, you will feel down and miserable because what you are administering into your subatomic quanta is weak confused energy that will jumble the flow of your waves of living thus allowing your whole physical, emotional, mental body to feel sick, in pain, down, anxiety, depressed, sad, miserable and in a state of chaos and confusion. But the moment you realize the reality that you are putting yourself in, you either change your mind about the situation you are in or go to someone else to help you cope with the state of your own manifested realty. You might solicit the help of an energy healer, or a physical doctor; but the doctor will give you medicine that can help the physical, and the energy healers give you energy or wave a crystal or use any technique to raise your energy. But, until you can create a new reality and realize that you have the power to change your subatomic waves, that forms your physical body particles, by downloading your own healing energy or by visiting a healer that can help you in understanding that the source of energy without you is the same power within you, your healing efforts will be a mere hit or miss.

So, what is this God Enhanced Healing Power? And how does it work? How can I adopt it, Can I make it bring me money, power to help other people?

I smiled at my student and said: No human needs your money and power to heal. You can heal humanity by your love. Money is not evil but an experience. Power is a self-tool to change your own energy to heal, rather than using it on others to manipulate their experience of their own healing. Money and power become evil only when it is used to enslave others to a certain way of operating their lives according to certain rules, regulations, rituals and dogmas under the fake assumption of healing and salvation.

Does that make sense? I addressed the student asking this question. She looked at me and shrugged her shoulder as if to say I do not know; and then I saw Suzanne my partner gave her a hug.

Before you indulge and go deeper into the Enhanced Healing Powers, let us understand some other basic terms that may help you as you start your journey of self-discovery and powerful healing.

What is the universe? The universe is defined as all existing matter in space and time as a whole, and all of energy in its various forms, including dark energy which is what holds life together, the essence of life, electromagnetic radiation, matter, waves and particles of the quanta, the subatomic energy of life that exist in the universe.

What is the universal healing energy? It is very important at this stage of self-healing to firmly understand that the Universal Energy is the energy that holds the known universe intact. Many teachers from the Far East, the Middle Ease and ancient Native American tribes utilized a form or another of this power to assist regular people in physical healing. In Tibet monks invented the "Chakras" the spinning wheels with prayers imprinted on them so that common people will spin the wheels and prayers will fly to the Gods on their behalf. Others in the Middle ease invented Sufism as means of appealing to the Gods. Others in the modern time such as Mikao Usui in the late 19th and early 20th century invented Reiki as means to understanding of how Jesus was able to heal. So Usui spent 21 days fasting on a mountain, which by the end of this seclusion he saw some symbols of ancient healing modalities, which he adopted for his new healing techniques and taught to special students. These teaching arrived in the USA and became so watered down and misrepresented. Yes, Reiki students can feel a certain energy moving through their bodies as they use certain symbols which they administer to clients by downloading this energy into their own body as conduits to the energy. But the whole source of Reiki was lost. What prevents Reiki from flowing naturally is the fact that Reiki practitioners are not taught that they are the source of this powerful energy, but the fact that they are an extension of the grand healing power. So, learning some symbols and waving it over the energy centers of the body can allow the receiver's energy to rise above the physical, and the receiver will feel well for a short time. But healing of the essence and the source of the energetic disturbance is not accomplished.

What is the Trinity of Creation? The essence of creation and the power you call the spirit of God, in our limited understanding as humans of what you can conceive God to be, is composed of three major energy essences that are intertwined in one creative power you call God. Great teachers through time immemorial taught us, as humans living on this spec at the outer realms of Milky Way you call earth, that the creative spirit of God is composed of a trinity of energies, Power, Wisdom and Love which is also transmitted as the essence of our creative trinity as humans living on this earth. Power is what is needed to influence creation, Wisdom to manage Creation, and Love to consciously cause it to happen. This enhanced healing energy works on all aspects of reality to help individuals to release their physical, emotional, mental pains and their internal choking energy; to help them create a different reality on this earthly journey.

So, could you please tell us how to become one with this God Universal Power to perform the Enhanced Healing Energy a student said with great enthusiasm?

The most important factor in enhancing your creative healing power is to acknowledge to yourself that you are an extension of God on earth. You must activate the God Triangle of creation within you; the triangle of power, wisdom and love. You must understand that you have infinite powers to create the grandest feelings you choose to manifest. That you are the God of your internal world with the capacity to create the way you function in this world. You create the frequency of your emotions, the capacity of your feelings. You create your total health and attitude, your belief system and your values in living. You create the way you respond to experiences and challenges in living. Your body responds to the way you think, feel and act. it is the power of your mind/body connection. When you are stressed, anxious or upset your body reacts in a way that might tell you that something isn't right. For example, you might develop high blood pressure or a stomach ulcer after a particularly stressful event, such as the death of a loved one.

The beliefs you hold about yourself and the world, your emotions, your memories, and your habits all can influence mental and physical health and can contribute to imbalances within the body. These connections between what is going on in your mind and heart, and what is happening in your body, form the psycho-emotional roots of health and disease. Emotions like anxiety can trigger increased stress hormones, which may suppress the immune system and set the stage for the development of infections or cancer. Science has begun to recognize the powerful connections through which emotional, spiritual, and behavioral factors can directly affect health outcomes. In fact, the type of vibrations or energy patterns that are carried by certain words and intentions can cause physical changes in DNA structure, which affect how the genetic code is translated to make different proteins that become the building blocks of your body. Therapies like hypnosis, visual imagery, meditation, yoga, biofeedback and Enhanced Reiki Healing Energy are being used to reestablish balance and promote health.

Knowing these facts, it is essential for you to start healing yourself. It essential for you to let the power of creation, the God Energy Powers of the universe, reactivate the God Energy Powers within your own cells. Emotions like anger, fear, guilt, anxiety, sadness, resentment, jealousy, depression, and stress will manifest within the body and contribute to imbalance and disease. Due to this mind body connection, the way you think and feel and the deep-seated belief patterns you hold can all contribute to the development of disease. If you do not explore and deal with painful emotions, they can create an underlying sense of anxiety, depression, or anger that can physically disrupt the body's natural ability to heal itself.

You must meditate to acknowledge that as humans you all have an embodied knowing of power as part of the cosmic intelligence and power; that there exists an innate and inherent healing intelligence within all of us that keep the atoms and the cells of our bodies functioning in an ideal atmosphere of healthy interactions.

So Old Man, what are the essential steps to be carried out by us on daily basis to feel the Great Powers of God within us, as Suzanne my partner looked at me and asked with a smile?

First: Meditating and understanding in every moment of your conscious living the power of the God Energy of the universe as one with the intricate part of the God Energy within your basic cells.

Second: Applying the power of self-Hypnosis while using self-encouraging positive and inspiring thoughts, emotions, and feelings which vibrate with the 95% God energy within your cell, which when said and felt, can change the basic data stored in your subconscious that has been causing free radical cells to cause disease and damaging feelings.

Third: Self Love. When you adjust your thoughts and emotions and fill your mind with the love of your heart, you will send vibrations that impact your cellular and overall physical state. Thus consciously using the grand awareness of your creative power in connection to the grand energy of God's creative energy, coupled with gentle words, thoughts and the grand unconditional feelings of Love for yourselves and the world, will activate your faith in your abilities to heal your own cellular free radical damage.

In short, with this approach of meditating the power of the creative energy of the universe coupled with the power of self-hypnosis, and self-love you begin to adjust to the inborn health within you and create the right conditions for it to flourish.

Please note: When assisting others that come for a healing treatment or using the non-personal approach, please always remember that you do not directly do the healing, but instead you create the conditions in which it can more easily occur by letting the person in your care to understand the healing power within themselves that is causing any change on their physical, emotional, mental or spiritual feelings.

Chapter Eleven

The God Within Me

Throughout all this book with the many questions and answers, and regardless of the ideas and solutions presented; there is a common denominator that must be recognized and adhered to.

Through my humble self, and through my teacher Steven, and through his teachers to the origin of life on this earth, there is an essential knowledge that has been passed from teacher to student, from mouth to ear. The Knowledge of The God Within. This knowledge has been distorted and many times forbidden by worldwide religions and religious groups and anti-religious institutions, regardless of which part of the world it belongs to.

Through science and the discovery of the world, and the discovery of the planets and galaxies scattered all over the universe, we are starting to understand that there is a power beyond the comprehension of science.

Electromagnetism runs what you can see, touch and feel known to scientists as the Ordinary Physical Matter and Ordinary Energy of the physical universe composes and run only 3% of the universe. On the other hand, the new study of the universe scientists agreed in the new standard Lambda-CDM model of cosmology that there is an unseen matter and energy that run 97% of the entire universal existence known as the Dark Matter and the Dark Energy. Dark does not mean it is evil. Dark means it is unknown, it has no light and cannot be seen. This unseen Dark Matter produces a gravitational attractive force that keeps the universe together, while the Dark Energy produces a repulsive force (antigravity) that is accelerating the universe at a fast-increasing rate of expansion. Together, they make up 97 % of the universe and you can't see either, but astronomers know that they exist.

Dark matter and dark energy are the yin and yang of the cosmos. Dark matter produces an attractive force (gravity), while dark energy produces a repulsive force (antigravity). They exist and are running the universe though you do not know what it is, but it has the most powerful effect on keeping the universe together as it is expanding at a great speed.

The atom inside a cell inside of a human being is a complete universe. The atom's Protons and Neutrons are the solid basis of an atom that pulls the atom together and allow it to expand. The stability of Protons is the (Dark Mater) that pulls the atom together, and the Electrons which keeps pulling away are driven by the (Dark Energy). Both powers inside a single atom of a cell in a human are the same projection of a human inside the universe outside.

A question was fired at me from the back of the class:

Where is God in all this talk and analysis?

I stopped for a moment as I remembered myself as a young boy firing the same question at my old teacher Steven. God, my dear, is this unseen power that holds the physical universe inside of every human and holds the outside universe together. God is not a man, a woman or a thing. God is not a jail keeper. God is not a man with an ego to satisfy. God is the power

SUHAIL S. JARROUSH PH.D.

of creation that keeps the outside world intact and the universe expanding, and at the same time keeps the universe inside of you intact as trillion upon trillions of atoms that compose the galaxies inside your body (your trillion and trillion cells) dye, split and being reborn on daily basis.

Thus, the God of creation the power of the Dark Matter and Energy that runs the universe and the multiverse with its trillions of galaxies and trillion upon trillions of stars is the same great God power of creation inside of each human. This power allows each one of us to create and control the movement of our atoms and cells inside our bodies which compose our systems and organs and the physical universe you call human beings.

I am a bit confused. You already told us before that God is Power, Wisdom and love, but all that you are now saying is that God is a power that creates the physical world. A student fired at me.

I smiled at this witty question and said: Yes, God to all the creations in this universe is all the Power, Wisdom and Love; and I assure you that you humans on this earth are not the only creative creatures in this vast universe. On this earth only there are millions of creations other that humans. All that I am concerned with at this junction of our teachings is to identify within each of us as humans living this earth. Maybe in another setting you will discuss what you call aliens or another species living on different stars in different galaxies, or the Anunnakis (The Gods that came from Heaven to earth). But for now, we will concentrate our discussions on humans on this earth as an extension of the external universal God Creator capable of all the attributes of what creation is all about.

Creation in a human form is a combination of the mind and the brain. The Brain is part of the visible, tangible world of the body that runs the body's physical organs and functions, while the Mind is the invisible power that transcendent the physical world as part of the universal creative power. The mind exists without the brain. The unseen power of the mind is not confined to the brain, but it interacts with the different parts of the brain to run the different aspects of the human physical functions.

The Mind:

1: Super Mind, the Creative Energy of God runs the combination of Dark energy and Dark matter which we cannot see, that together make up 97% of the universe and the physical body.

2: Conscious Mind, the human awake state of experiences and judgment.

3: Subconscious Mind, the automatic repetitive creation from past data.

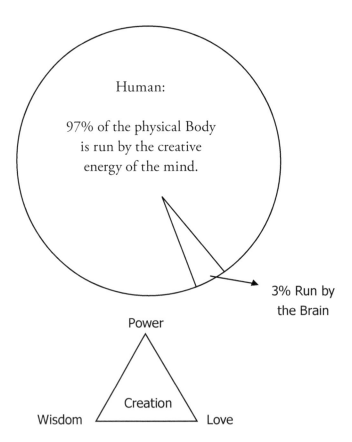

The Mind's **Creative Power** is divided into three attributes, when applied together will create wonders.

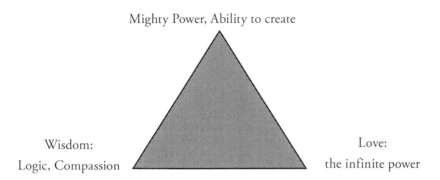

Mighty Power, Ability to create

Wisdom:
Logic, Compassion

Love:
the infinite power

Power to create: The human mind creative connection to the universal invisible Creative Mind, known as the Dark Energy and Matter that runs the existence and movement of the universe. Working on a smaller scale with every human brain to keep the physical function of all human atoms and cells intact, especially cells splitting, dying, rebirth and growth until the next cycle of creation.

Wisdom to create: Wisdom the combination of logic and compassion is driven by the invisible energy of the mind. Wisdom is the source of the invisible mystical world of all thought, feeling, attitude, belief, imagination and behavior. The mind allows humans to solve complicated logical problems. You cannot see someone thinking, nor can you observe their emotions, or memories, or perceptions and dreams. But Our mind's ability to analyze situations makes it possible for us to develop practical solutions to our problems such as anxiety, fear, panic, hurt etc. and lead us toward practical solutions. This creative energy of the mind engages the brain to affect the physical welfare of the human body through all the turmoil of our embedded ancient stories. The mind allows humans to reach a logical conclusion consistent with what you consider to be true for many years of our lives. Through our consistent operation of logic and compassion, our irrational and unfounded delusions will always give way to wisdom.

Power of Love: The third aspect of the Power of Creation is Love. Love is the powerful freedom of limitless existence that resides within every human on this earth and beyond. It is the catalyst that binds might and wisdom to become the gentle power of infinite possibilities of thinking and feeling. Love is the power that allows us to gently recognize our self-worth, our values and beliefs, and allows us to work on changing ourselves as you choose to be without judgment, conditions or expectations. In simplicity, Love is freedom.

My friends, the greatest message I will leave you with is for you to start to recognize that no single existence on this earth, or on trillion of trillion existences all over the universe, is a separate existence by itself. From the smallest subatomic life in every creature on this earth to the grandest universe and Multiverse are one unit of being, and for lack of total knowledge and understanding of the name, you call the being God.

The great power of the individual mind works with the brain to organize the creation and expiration of the human cells and to restore harmony to the individual being when in disharmony. At the same instant as the human mind is restoring the physical being, it is also communicating with the universal mind relaying and receiving data of restoration or alignment of the physical body. Every human and every living being on the earth is a unique cell in the whole body of the universe. And what happens on the physical world is reflected in the universe which is the unknown body of God. As the intelligence of the individual cell in my body has no idea of the totality of who I am as a total being, but works independently using the power of its mind, which is connected to my mind, to create itself to split and die and to be reborn in my body, the same happens to me as an individual cell in the body of the universe you call God. I use my mind to create the grandest feelings I can as I grow, live and die as a cell in body of the God the universe.

Old man, what you are saying is very profound. It sounds great but it is a farfetched idea. I cannot believe that I and God are one, for I pray to God for help. So how about the angels and the arch angels and Maryam the gentle power that you say touches the back of your hair to calm you down, and Steven your teacher, though dead, he always speaks in your head? I love the idea that God and I are one, but could you please explain all that to me, I am really confused. A student fired at me.

I smiled and said: My dear this class is over for tonight. But I assure you that we will discuss this subject and many other subjects in the classes to follow. But for now, I enjoyed you being in my class listening to me, and allowing me the opportunity to disclose to you some of the ancient knowledge that has been taught from teacher to student, from mouth to ear, since the beginning of time to the end of what is now, and the beginning of whatever it will be. But before I leave you tonight, I will leave you with this thought that will be the basis for our future discussions.

(The moment you are born you are entrusted with a whole universe to develop and run; so, what universe are you creating).

See you soon.

Suhail S. Jarroush
The Old Man"

My Peace I give you,
But my love is there for you to take.

Printed in the United States
By Bookmasters